# Women of the PITS

## of the

### Shattering the Glass Ceiling in Financial Markets

**MARA KOPPEL**

**Dearborn**
**Financial Publishing, Inc.®**

This publication is designed to provide accurate and authoritative information in regard to the subject matter covered. It is sold with the understanding that the publisher is not engaged in rendering legal, accounting, or other professional service. If legal advice or other expert assistance is required, the services of a competent professional person should be sought.

Editoral Director: Cynthia A. Zigmund
Managing Editor: Jack Kiburz
Interior Design: Lucy Jenkins
Cover Design: S. Laird Jenkins Corporation
Typesetting: Debra Lenyoun
Cover Photo: Courtesy of the Chicago Board of Trade

Published by Dearborn Financial Publishing, Inc.®

Printed in the United States of America

98  99  00  10  9  8  7  6  5  4  3  2  1

**Library of Congress Cataloging-in-Publication Data**

Koppel, Mara.
    Women of the pits : shattering the glass ceiling of financial
markets / by Mara Koppel.
        p.   cm.
    ISBN 0-7931-2737-8
        1. Women in finance—United States—Biography.   2. Women
stockbrokers—United States—Biography.   3. Women in finance—
Promotions—United States—Case studies.   I. Title.
    HD6073.F472U65   1998
    332.6'082'092273—dc21                                        98-29916
    [B]                                                                    CIP

Dearborn books are available at special quantity discounts to use as premiums and sales promotions, or for use in corporate training programs. For more information, please call the Special Sales Manager at 800-621-9621, ext. 4384, or write to Dearborn Financial Publishing, Inc., 155 North Wacker Drive, Chicago, IL 60606-1719.

# Foreword

Mara Koppel's new book, *Women of the Pits: Shattering the Glass Ceiling in Financial Markets,* is a timely volume, arriving as the financial services industry is going through perhaps its most profound period of change ever.

These changes are impacting not only what types of products and services are being offered in the marketplace, but also how those products and services are developed, structured, marketed, and delivered. The people who work day-to-day in financial services are also changing. It is this change that is at the heart of Mara Koppel's book.

The futures and options business, like may industries and professions before it, is experiencing a steady influx of women. What makes these stories particularly worthwhile are the futures industry's gridironlike intensity level and the tenacity of the women profiled. Their success is testament to the plain fact that persistence and sheer determination can crumble even seemingly insurmountable barriers. These stories clearly show that being able to summon the smarts, will, and tenacity to survive and thrive in the sometimes unforgiving trading pits is by no means an exclusively male trait.

Through 15 finely detailed profiles, Koppel delves into the lives of a diverse group of women who each brings a unique history as she enters her trading career. And each ultimately discovers—on her own terms—an inner drive that keeps her repeatedly challenging the pitfalls of the marketplace.

Along the way, these women learn that the barriers presumed to come with the territory are not nearly as formidable as they may have expected. Nor are these barriers nearly as important to the characters as confronting their own inner obstacles, which are met and conquered through various means.

There is an interesting diversity among the women profiled. Sharon King experienced a tragic childhood on Chicago's impoverished South Side that taught her the street smarts to become a player in stock options at the Chicago Board Options Exchange. Leslie Henner Burns, who made her mark in the Chicago Mercantile Exchange's Standard & Poor's 500 pit, was a third-generation trader in her family and still the first woman. And Mei Ping Yang, an ethnic Chinese woman who frequently faced discrimination growing up in Malaysia, used her multinational upbringing to good effect, helping her develop the skills necessary to trade simultaneously in numerous markets.

The book also highlights the various paths that lead to Chicago's financial pits. Though some of the book's subjects are from families for whom trading has been a tradition, there also are those who happened on the business through such random routes as blind newspaper advertisements.

Not unlike their male counterparts, the characters here often came to trading after first having explored other career options. With educational and work backgrounds ranging from particle physics to interpretive dance, these women find the energy of the trading pits an apt metaphor for life in all its various incarnations.

Yet what unifies the very different characters of *Women of the Pits* is the sense of spiritual growth that each experiences following years of surviving the wrenching turns of the financial markets. To a person, the characters profiled here all found that even more than financial rewards, which are "only the way of keeping score," as one woman states, were the emotional rewards of having survived this most demanding of professions.

It is this personal growth that will stay with the reader long after the book is finished. I sincerely hope that *Women of the Pits* will convince even more women to join the ranks of those female traders who have gone before them.

—T. Eric Kilcollin
President and CEO, Chicago Mercantile Exchange

# Acknowledgments

I wish to thank the remarkable and resourceful women who generously shared their time and their lives, allowing themselves to be known.

I'll never forget any of them and I expect my readers won't either. It is my sincere desire that Roslyn Abell, Ann Berg, Leslie Henner Burns, Arlene Busch, Jenny Costello, Janet Disteldorf, Karen Doherty, Carol Hancock, Katherine Harig, Sharon King, Mary MacDiarmid, Robin Mesch, Mickey Norton, Jennifer Strausberg, and Mei Ping Yang enjoy reading about themselves and each other as much as I enjoyed shaping their stories into this book.

Without the understanding of my family there would be no book. Thanks to Bob for steadfast encouragement and to Lily and Niko for eating all that pizza and not bugging me about the myriad details of daily life that are always ready to evaporate those creative juices.

In addition, I wish to thank Howard Abell and Nora Chiriboga for their invaluable technical assistance. This book has been a tremendous learning experience for me as I hope it will prove for many others.

Thanks also go to my editor Cynthia Zigmund and the entire staff at Dearborn Financial Publishing for their generous support of this project.

# Contents

"I used to be Snow White but I drifted."

—Mae West, American film actress

# Preface

I feel I know commodities traders very well. Despite state-of-the-art technology and the global herding ground, traders are an endangered species. Their most prominent characteristic, which is absolutely basic to everything they do and believe in, is their sense of, and quest for, independence. Like the buffalo, they prefer to run free as they graze in their particular stretch of the financial range. This is not easily accomplished with increasing regulation—often necessary—and the astronomical and sometimes prohibitive costs of memberships known as "seats." Ironically, the owners of what are actually licenses spend most of their time on their feet yelling and gesturing like natives of primitive tribes attempting to communicate.

The entire enterprise of trading commodities is about communicating a particular idea or response to something traders have spied in the overwhelming flow of information that darts electronlike around the globe. It can best be understood as active communication, a "conversation" between a buyer and a seller. It is ironic that our late 20th century means of communication has one foot and an arm based in the ancient past of gesture, intimidation, and face-to-face confrontation with the adversary, and the other foot linked to the world by an IV of cutting-edge technology that has truly outdistanced many predictions made by science fiction. The trader is positioned at the interface of primordial gesture and futuristic science in an almost comic as well as cosmiclike energy burst and information flow.

The trader is positioned at the interface of primordial gesture and futuristic science in an almost comic as well as cosmiclike energy burst and information flow.

It is ironic that the actors who understand the trading process, which is complex and at the same time crazy, are a unique band of individuals who utterly believe in themselves and their hard-earned skill of "reading" the seeming chaos and responding with resolute confidence. If these "players" of the global marketplace are right, they get to stay in the game and move on. If they err, they're brought down, and if they fail to correct their course, cast out. Successful survival requires the constant and draining dusting-off and picking-oneself-up-again process and reclaiming one's spot and role. Darwin would recognize what is happening.

If this sounds like a bizarre, high-speed version of musical chairs, you are beginning to get the picture. It is an extremely unforgiving drama that requires total dedication and concentration. A momentary distraction or poorly considered decision can cost everything.

There are also long periods of calm. Like ancient mariners, traders wait for some bit of news to billow their financial sails and send them breezily on to a pleasing destination.

As the wife of a professional commodities trader, I've spent a lot of time in these shark-infested waters. I've had considerable time to reflect while treading water and hoping for a speedy rescue. I also remember periods of drought when previously vital areas were transformed into tomblike expanses.

---

As the wife of a professional commodities trader, I've

spent a lot of time in these shark-infested waters. I've

had considerable time to reflect while treading water

and hoping for a speedy rescue.

---

The periods of distress have provided great opportunities for studying the nature and behavior of individual traders. Although they share some characteristics, one can honestly say that no two are alike.

Those who practice trading see it as a, if not *the*, last frontier where, despite regulation, globalization, and automation, there is still space. Space in the sense of opportunity where it is not only possible but expected to be able to make a good living working for yourself. The main requirement is unflinching belief in oneself and the ability to keep battering away at all costs. Only the strong-willed need apply.

If you have a good day, you can take full credit, but you are responsible for the bad days as well. It takes a unique person who can live with risk and uncertainty and keep going even in highly negative situations. Sturdy feet and a good set of lungs help. Despite all the screens, computers, and everything else, the trading field is populated by colonies differentiated by colored cotton jackets gesturing frantically and yelling wildly. All the while hoping they got it right. It is completely weird and is, let's face it, an utterly primitive society going through its rites. Instead of priests reading chicken gizzards, color-coded people are racing to decipher symbols that are constantly changing as a result of their interaction with a universe of other vital factors.

It is absolutely amazing that this vast and astonishing "big top" works as well as it does. It is a dizzying dance of constantly altering choreography and participants engaged in a mysterious and crucial global pageant.

What I've described should convey a sense of the ceaseless drama that surges on the financial stages and shores around the world. I've been through it all. We've played all the parts. The sudden move from golden luxury to what resembled a shark feeding ground. There were also occasions whose unexpected chill recalled the last moments of the *Titanic*. My only thought at these times was whether we would make it to the lifeboat. There was the panic-based question whether there even was a boat. In addition, there was real concern about whether it was seaworthy and equipped for a voyage of undetermined duration.

During and after the struggle to survive, there is time to study this crazy business of trading; what it requires, and the massive toll it exacts. Trading is like no other profession I can think of other than dragon slaying. Facing that hot breath and those toothy jaws fearlessly, armed only with belief in oneself, on a daily basis.

Why would *anyone* choose to build a career on a constantly shifting and treacherous field—an apt description of a financial market? One can also view it as a black hole that exists and grows by sucking in matter.

My trader-writer husband has studied and written about the men who engage in this financial contest. Through my involvement as sounding board for his books, I have become a fellow "trader watcher" and observer of this unique culture. What are those qualities a few possess that enable them to scale market heights, ride out surges, and recover from the lows? Why do some choose to skydive, soar, scale hostile mountains or market faces while others seek easier and more secure comfort? What sort of person is attracted to this risky but rewarding energy field?

In this relatively small group of men appears the occasional, lone female trader—the individual who is the basis of this book. What drew her to this high-intensity world and what is there in backbone and nerves that enables her to thrive and succeed in one of the most stress-laden and demanding occupations imaginable?

By any standards, women traders are a remarkable group of high achievers in a league with other pioneers. They belong with the adventurous, not only in spirit, but in sustained action in any high-skill, high-risk, high-velocity area. I feel we have a great deal to learn from their focus, persistence, and work ethic. They are extra-ordinarily independent and self-reliant. I believe there is much to harvest from their thinking and activity, both of which are powered by a solid and uncompromising belief in themselves.

Despite a growing number of books and articles, the general public's view of a trader is still of someone who does far too little work for too great a reward, is engaged in a somewhat shady area, and deserves the all too frequently reported tragic fall. The stereotypical trader is usually imagined to be someone who drives a fast and expensive car, wears a watch with too many functions, and shops for material possessions at a rate at which others buy groceries.

*Women of the Pits* presents the real person. Books have been written about professional women who have established themselves and made it on Wall Street and other financial streets at various distances from that famous glass ceiling we hear much about. Even on the most pressured day, they can take a breath, push a button, and check on their nanny from a corner office on a high floor. They are surrounded by a support network and occupy a relatively defined role with established rules and understandable expectations. There is breathing room between them and their work.

Some do take a few swings at that ceiling and others have gotten too comfortable.

Trading is different. Traders, the many males and rarer females, are cheek by jowl, jacket to jacket in what, for good reason, are called the pits. The ascent is difficult, the activity tumultuous, the pressure intense, and the company rough. The descent can be unexpected and swift, and the landing on the bottom perilous and terrifying. The entire experience can be pretty unforgiving. Does it sound like fun? Or what an ideal work situation is made of?

What I have described is routine in the trader's life. On a daily basis she is engaged by choice in an uncertain, risk-driven profession that is sensitive to whatever is bothering the world at that moment. It can be the health of livestock in England, chicken maladies exported from China, or the private romantic lives of world leaders. All contribute to the ebb and flow of the world's financial tides.

Imagine a vast sea composed of the fruits of the world's economies, representing the work of billions of people engaged in all manner of activities ranging from farming to cutting-edge technofinancial colonies. There is something insectlike and organic about it, as all flows into ever greater currents of information circling the globe as ceaselessly as the oceans, picking up matter wherever it goes and changing in often unpredictable ways.

It is all this information that the trader has to read, understand, and act on with lightning swiftness and laserlike focus. What impact, if any, will some event in a place whose name is unfamiliar and unpronounceable have? How does too little or too much rainfall or sunshine affect a price for the next year or longer?

It's fascinating and at the same time mindboggling. Despite the instant information and move toward globalization, the average person seems to prefer and yearn for a calmer and more predictable existence. We hear about those individuals who accumulate great wealth so they can chuck it all and eventually live the "simple life" on several hundred acres.

Each of the women you are about to meet is dedicated to her career decision and continues to design and fine-tune her work and life to her specifications. These women have worked incredibly hard to have power over how they live their life. Yet they are wise and realistic enough to accept that something can always cause an abrupt break in what moments ago seemed so certain.

I feel we have much to learn from how each one has handled the demands and pressures of her exceedingly precarious chosen profession and has also managed to lead a real life.

One of the most valuable lessons I've learned from spending almost a quarter century around traders and trading is to never give up. There's always another day, another opportunity. Duke Ellington's observation on success could well describe a good trading day: "It's doing the right thing at the right time under the right conditions in front of the right people." As you read each interview, watch out for the fine rain of glass from the high ceiling above. Also, don't be afraid to step over the jagged pieces lying on the trading floor. You are about to find out how they got there!

———————————

Duke Ellington's observation on success could well

describe a good trading day: "It's doing the right

thing at the right time under the right conditions in

front of the right people."

———————

This book is dedicated to the women whose stories it tells and to those who will find inspiration and courage in them to believe in themselves and their ability to achieve their goals.

# CHAPTER 1

# Beyond the
# Glass Screen

"If you don't go out in the woods, nothing will ever
happen and your life will never begin."—Unknown

On the surface this book may appear to be about traders and trading, but it is really about the enduring strength of the human spirit.

You are about to meet an extraordinary group of women. Each unique story could belong to no one else. Each woman has entered the "financial woods" armed with her wits and experience. Each one is on a "vision quest," to borrow a crucial concept from Native Americans, which requires total dedication to the undertaking and absolute self-knowledge. The insights of these women into their own character will help us to understand their motivation and drives.

These are female traders and financial experts who have chosen one of the most demanding occupations imaginable. We will discover why each was drawn to this profession of extremes and what made it possible for her to take the harrowing turns at breakneck speed with little protection at what can best be described as financial luge.

The trading world is a high-wire act of brains, precision, and nerves of steel. We will trace the sources of strength that these women draw on to succeed in an arena that requires the persistence of a Mother Teresa, the energy level of a Tina Turner, and the steadfastness of the Statue of Liberty. All of this takes place at the edge of chaos. Day in, day out.

———————

We will trace the sources of strength that these women draw on to succeed in an arena that requires the persistence of a Mother Teresa, the energy level of a Tina Turner, and the steadfastness of the Statue of Liberty. All of this takes place at the edge of chaos. Day in, day out.

———

It will become clear why trading was the right match for these women who operated at various distances from the arena's center: in the pit, along its rims, or, in the case of two traders from "upstairs." This is a highly intelligent group that attended a wide range of schools where they did very well in a variety of majors. Not one went to a business school, and one just missed being sent to reform school.

Their work background ranges from a 411 operator to cocktail waitress and a muskrat trapper and skinner! There was also a former corn shucker and a census worker.

All social levels are represented—working class, middle class, and upper class—and one trader who was raised in an orphanage and foster home. In every case there was someone who valued the future trader as an individual. In some cases it was an entire family; for others it was a strong but unrelated role model. Each woman knew what her life and effort were worth. Even when she hadn't actually proven herself, she had a strong image of her potential and placed a high value on herself. All the women are lifelong learners.

Not surprisingly, all the traders gave credit to their family for supporting them and believing in them, although they were often embarking in a direction that no one else in the family had chosen. Time and time again I heard how a parent's encouragement was taken to heart. A constant refrain was the memory of being told there was nothing that couldn't be accomplished if they put their minds to it. In only one instance was trading viewed as a move in the wrong direction toward an uncertain future.

Although the path to their chosen career was sometimes indirect, there did seem to be a strong progression—sometimes through less challenging and lower-level jobs—until the goal was finally attained. In one case the goal was a midlife event after the first child had started school.

All of the women were extremely hardworking. No matter what their background, there was no question that they would lead productive lives requiring a lot of input. Not just any job would do. It definitely needed to be one that was challenging and demanding. One woman promised herself that she would be a trader by the age of 30. If that didn't work out, plan B was to head for Hollywood and have her own comedy show, à la Roseanne. Another waited until her last child entered first grade. They were all ambitious when the time was right.

On-the-job training was often no more than training by the seat of the pants. The essential feature was alertness and a willingness to learn. Despite considerable obstacles, including the "closed shop" that confronted several pioneers who opened doors, they made it through sheer determination, will, and professionalism.

Throughout their male-dominated environment, the women could have given up or yelled, "Harassment." They chose to keep things in balance and didn't allow distractions to divert them from their mission.

Across the board they sought out, and were attracted to, extremely demanding work. Specifically, they all ended up in an area that provided the independence they sought.

If we think of the trading world as the last frontier, these strong-willed individuals possess the pioneer spirit and energy to be able to navigate choppy waters. Not only have they crossed physical frontiers, they have not hesitated to pass psychological boundaries. One trader is a former debutante; another came from a large struggling working-class family and has achieved a life offering choices for her children. There's a doctor's daughter and a newsstand proprietor's daughter. Each has a background that in some way has contributed to who she is, whether by taking advantage of it or reacting against it and reaching out for something else.

———————— ■ ————————

All were pointed toward a dynamic world that runs on brains, guts, and timing. Some paths were more direct than others. Some went directly to it in a few purposeful moves. Others took several trips around the game board and experienced unexpected delays.

But they all made it.

————————

All of these women have also crossed cultural, social, and in one case racial boundaries. Not one was prepared to settle for less. Each did it on her own without relying on litigation or influence groups. All were pointed toward a dynamic world that runs on brains, guts, and timing. Some paths were more direct than others. Some went directly to it in a few purposeful moves. Others took several trips around the game board and experienced unexpected delays. But they all made it.

What unites them all—no matter their origin, education, or experience—is their strength of character and confidence. Their stories reveal how they have succeeded. We will learn what they have gained and learned about themselves through their experiences and how they put this knowledge to work.

Several of them were first in their fields and are in fact legendary. The list includes the first woman to hold a membership at the Chicago Mercantile Exchange. Another was the first to actively trade at the Chicago Board of Trade. Another is the only African-American member of the Chicago Board Options Exchange. Still another was elected twice to the male-dominated board of directors of the Chicago Board of Trade.

Each woman claimed an area, defended it, and grew within it, making it prosper. Not one paid any attention to those who said they couldn't do it or it couldn't be done. That sort of statement had absolutely no meaning for these women other than serving to urge them on. In other words, they were unstoppable when it came to achieving their goals.

They had a vision of themselves and their abilities and just stuck with it. In the words of one, "I could hang on forever. I would never give up." Another said, "You just keep going." In the words of Scarlett O'Hara at the end of *Gone With the Wind*, "Tomorrow is another day."

Their competence and professionalism have seen these women through. Who are these remarkable characters and how have they adapted to the rigorous terrain they have chosen? If you're picturing someone who looks like a kick boxer or a member of a motorcycle gang, you're in for a surprise. In general, they are on the petite and slender side. One exception was a six-footer. All are fully engaged in their life. One works to be able to come home and hang out with her children. Another's ideal getaway is Disney World. One even worked in a back brace after surgery.

You may expect these women to be loud and overly aggressive to compete with their male colleagues. They don't eat nails for breakfast! They tend to be soft spoken, although they assured me they had no trouble making themselves heard. One went to a voice coach to learn how to project her voice like an opera singer hitting the high notes.

In the course of the interviews, the women conveyed a dynamic reserve that suggested the ability to spring into action, mentally and physically, in a tick if they had to. They are all high energy. Even when not working, they are busy with activities such as working with the homeless, teaching disadvantaged youth, and supporting sports activities. They aren't found clearing out luxury stores or living particularly extravagantly, although they all live well: Their career choice has expanded their life choices and presented them with more options than they might have had if they had become involved in some other area.

These are strong women. They have not found it necessary or even desirable to imitate men or outdo them to prove themselves. They don't have to. They don't understand the reluctance, more like the terror, that prevents many women from becoming traders.

All were eager to tell their story for several reasons. First—and the reason for this book—they are great stories. Some are Dickens-like, others are filled with adventure. All are dramatic. The common element is unflinching confidence in their ability to do it and face the fire. This is a very nourishing quality. Each instance of success or striving builds and strengthens.

As you are about to learn, the women love telling their story: the hardships overcome, courses set, and goals achieved. Their hope is that these "trader tales" will encourage more women to enter this field with confidence and understanding—a field that can provide tremendous excitement and an excellent, if uneven, living for the independent minded.

These are individuals who can juggle activities physically and mentally. These women tend to be good at organizing and keeping a lot of things going at once. This is a skill that is transferable to the financial field where it is necessary to have perfect focus while keeping in mind a vast amount of information.

The subject of ego also came up. Speaking from experience, they tended to think that women on the whole behave in less ego-driven ways than men. This is especially crucial at those times when it's like a bad day in the ER. The profits keep hemorrhaging, and there's a pervasive sense of near panic combined with a helpless feeling. Sometimes nothing can be done but, in the words of one, "end the pain," clean up the blood, take a deep breath, and move on.

It is at these times in this human crucible that things can get really exciting. The tough get going while others take it personally. Going down with the ship is not recommended. The market is not stalking anyone in particular, although it often seems that way. Incredible stories abound about what is a really bad day and how it gets handled.

Even so, after the really bad day, there is the next day. How does that work? Is it really a new day or is it a continuation of its disappointing predecessor? It takes a certain kind of person to go at it day after day, especially during a losing streak. It is important to remember if you're in the circus that sometimes it's necessary for even a high-wire artist to pitch some hay for the elephants or shovel some droppings. It's show biz! "Pitching and shoveling" are part of trading, and sometimes it's necessary to do whatever it takes to survive. The important thing is survival and return. It can't always be a good day. Like life itself, trading takes a lot of effort and keeping your eye on your goal.

The trading floor is a sea of color and seeming chaos, but those who stay and study can read it like the Talmud—the authoritative body of Jewish tradition. When something unusual happens, there is always some sharp "tack" who can find a reference point or previous example or singularity.

You have probably realized by now that trading is a very difficult field. It is also true that for the most part those who have chosen this work really can't wait to do it. They get up early like newspaper delivery boys used to in the old days to stand in a relatively small area as crowded as the subway during rush hour. Like the subway, there is no first class section and everyone travels in steerage. No preferential seating is available, and it's necessary to stand the entire way, which in the case of trading can mean six hours without a break. If you are in front of a screen, you don't want to leave it even to go to the bathroom. That could just be the time you miss some crucial piece of information that's going to make or break your day. Strong kidneys and strong everything else are good when it comes to trading!

———————————————

Like the subway, there is no first class section and

everyone travels in steerage. No preferential seating

is available, and it's necessary to stand the entire way,

which in the case of trading can mean six hours

without a break.

————

There's shoving, pencil poking, foot stomping, falling off a step, fainting. There is vocabulary that mothers wouldn't like to hear. There have been heart attacks. Ears have been bitten! There have even been untimely deaths. This should give you a pretty accurate picture of what these women have chosen to contend with.

There are no windows in the pits, just dizzying volumes of numbers that would probably stun Einstein. Everything is constantly changing. It's up to each player what she chooses to select out of the buzzing hive of information. Each instant brings a new decision to be made. Tick. Tick. Like time itself. It's filling each second with purposeful activity. In the words of one, "It's better to be a player than a prayer." As the old trading expression goes, "Bulls make money; bears make money; pigs get slaughtered."

---

There are no windows in the pits, just dizzying volumes of numbers that would probably stun Einstein. Everything is constantly changing. It's up to each player what she chooses to select out of the buzzing hive of information.

---

Trading is a vibrant theater of human nature that exacts top performance on a daily basis. Anything else has a negative and costly consequence. Nobody's perfect and personal weaknesses are always under review. As one trader reminded me, "The road to success is always under construction."

How do the players hurl themselves into the trading arena time and time again? What personal methods have they developed to cope with the extreme chronic pressures of this madcap, but all too serious, world? It is said it's a "hard way to make an easy buck!" Stress management is essential and each woman has had to develop a constructive way of dealing with her days, good as well as bad, even disastrous ones. Each is functioning in a financial bloodbath and needs to be prepared for any unexpected catastrophe.

One trader relaxes by watching her favorite cartoons! Another meditates to return to a place of calm after experiencing the chaos of the marketplace. Another creates exquisite and complex multi-layered works of art combining delicacy and strength, light and dark. One spends time with her children. Another, a professional sports team owner, is a devoted game follower. There's even one who enjoys training as a boxer, throwing crisp, lethal punches at a boxing bag in her home!

Each does something that is effective and provides a change of pace from the rigors of the day. Each knows it is necessary to enter a peaceful state and restore herself. All possess the ability to replenish their psychic and physical energy to their critical level before reentering the zone once more. As traders, they are constantly traveling between high-pitched intensity levels, working out ways of handling the abrupt psychological change in positive ways. Enough introduction, let's hear the stories of their well-lived and well-worked lives.

# CHAPTER 2

# Number One

## CAROL "MICKEY" NORTON

No sooner was it known that I was planning this project than I heard that I had to talk to Carol Norton. I knew about the legendary "Mickey," as she is known. A true pioneer, she was the first woman pit trader in the newly created IMM (international monetary market) at the Chicago Mercantile Exchange. In addition, she was probably the first female trader in Chicago. Extending the circle, there is ample reason to think of her as the first female trader in America. And no one has come forward to challenge the claim that she may well have been the first female pit trader in the world!

Knowing this, I didn't know what to expect when I contacted her. There was no voice mail or message machine. The hoarse voice on the other end greeted me like an old friend. I heard about her soon-to-arrive first grandchild and her former husband's recovery from a heart attack. I got a very favorable impression of a woman who was totally involved with others and not preoccupied with maintaining her image. In other words, Mickey had more important things to do than polish her trophies.

Despite a serious cold, she was flying to Paris the following day to attend an exhibition game of her beloved Chicago Bulls. An avid sportswoman and fan, she is a part owner of the Bulls as well as of the White Sox. We made plans to meet on her return. Jet lag was never mentioned.

On the appointed day, I found myself delayed by downtown traffic on a rainy morning. I finally reached Mickey's home, which interestingly is equidistant between her two major passions outside of her family: the Chicago Mercantile Exchange and the United Center, home of the Bulls. After passing through a series of levels and doors and wondering if I would be able to find my car again, I rang her bell.

I was greeted like a close friend by a slender woman. Her perfectly and recently done hair and nails contrasted with her Bulls-emblazoned warm-up suit. The spring in her step was not entirely due to her spotless white gym shoes. Around her neck was a big Bulls championship pendant and on her finger was the same ring the players received!

Her most remarkable feature was her face with its kind and interested expression. Her alert, slightly wry eyes had a definite sparkle. We settled down beside each other on a soft couch. She told me she had recently moved from a house and had compacted its contents into this much smaller high-rise apartment. We were surrounded by an impressive array of sports memorabilia and fine oriental antiques bumping up against each other.

A personalized signed photograph of Dennis Rodman wearing a dress kept watch over us, vying with antique lacquered furniture, rare porcelain, and Asian art. In addition, Mickey kept a handheld Quotron in her palm, which she frequently checked to see how her various positions in the markets were doing. It reminded me of a doctor checking a pulse. It was a confluence of finance and sports and other elements that would be brought into clear focus during the course of the morning. I should also mention this was a day the Dow dropped 90 points, but, as with everything else, she took it in her stride and continued with her story.

These periodic movements are usually unexpected and are opportunities for major financial losses, if not ruin. I felt like I was at home with a fabled Hall of Famer whose trades and "market plays" have gone into the record books and are still talked about.

We got started. It was an easy, chatty interview with this woman who was first in her chosen "court" as the Bulls have been in theirs. Only she was on her own and had to play all the positions herself.

This "den mother" to the Bulls hardly started out with trading in her sights. A physician's daughter, Mickey was raised on Chicago's posh Lake Shore Drive. After attending public schools, she graduated from the University of Illinois at the age of 18 with a degree in mathematics. "My only previous business experience occurred in college when I had a scarf concession and was the campus Revlon rep!" She was also junior editor of the yearbook and vice president of the YMCA.

Her lifelong love of sports grew from attending games with her father. Her father played an enduring role in her life, continuing to inspire her, and she credits him as the source of her strength and self-confidence. They were very close, and she regretted that he did not live to see his first grandchild.

After college, she worked as an actuary before going to Washington, D.C., where she was the legislative assistant to a senator from Pennsylvania. She remembers dancing with Bobby Kennedy and would have liked to have gone into politics as another career choice. At that time, she couldn't see herself spending her life in an area where advancement for women was unknown. Although after hearing her story, I would have been surprised if she had persisted and not succeeded.

She got married and had three children. During this time, she played bridge with a group that included Leo Melamed, who is known as the founding father of the financial futures industry. This game proved to be a "bridge" to her subsequent career. She was a first-rate bridge player. Time and again, Leo would suggest that Mickey buy an exchange seat and start trading. "My constant refrain was, 'Don't be silly!'"

She and her husband had made some investments in grain that she scrupulously followed. Mickey has always thought of money as the ultimate commodity and has specialized in trading currencies, particularly the British pound.

The price had risen from $5,000 to $10,000 for an IMM seat and to $50,000 for the fully loaded Chicago Mercantile Exchange (Merc) membership by the time she finally relented. Her youngest child had just entered first grade. "To this day, one of my few regrets is that I didn't buy a seat earlier at the lower price." She doesn't like to waste money or to be off on her timing.

Mickey and Leo made a deal. He would teach her to trade. She would help him become a life master in bridge, a goal that he achieved. After three lessons, including some charting, Mickey was ready to start trading. After being recommended for membership and passing a series of exams, she made $70 on her first trade. To her mind, she was off and trading! All in all, it was a good trade!

When asked why she and trading made a good match, Mickey replied that she had been a math major and felt at home with numbers. "It never occurred to me that I couldn't do it!"

In her own words, "I took to trading like a duck to water." Her guts and intuition helped her stay afloat in the "pond." "My stomach told me when to get into a trade, and my stomach told me when it was time to get out!"

---

"I took to trading like a duck to water." Her guts and intuition helped her stay afloat in the "pond."

Mickey doesn't see herself as overly competitive and prefers to share. She doesn't have any desire to, or see any need to, push someone around. "I like to take other people up with me." In fact, her husband joined her trading for a short period, but it wasn't for him. She always did better and "was flying." She gave all of her children an IMM seat on their 21st birthday. One son is a trader.

Her badge symbol, "Micky," is unique. It is the only one that has five letters. She got her nickname at birth when family members thought she favored an uncle named Mickey. Curiously, she admits she never learned the hand signals and would tap traders on the shoulder or poke them in the back to get their attention. To this day, she is not certain what a tick is in each of the commodities she trades. Not especially loud, she once brought a megaphone to the floor, which wasn't allowed at the time but is now. None of this stopped her progress or slowed her down. She was busy learning the behavior of what she was trading and what she could do with it.

After the grueling workday, Mickey still had enough energy left to unwind. She would take a couple aerobics classes, run the track, and spend some time on the treadmill. On days when the market went against her, the only thing she could do until the following day was go to sleep. Sometimes she would take time off and spend an afternoon on the golf course. "You really have to leave it." She always tried to do something positive even on those aptly named "black" days. All in all, "I couldn't wait for tomorrow. It was always exciting." It's no wonder she has kept that feeling going by her involvement with the Bulls through their six championships. She has a ring for each winning season and enough personal memorabilia to open up a substantial gift shop!

Mickey has always believed the mind is like a minicomputer, and she likes to keep hers actively engaged at all times. A very optimistic person, she takes in all the information that is coming in and then makes up her own mind. Her response to my question about difficulties she may have encountered evoked a response as if she were hearing a foreign concept: "What difficulties!" She does admit to sometimes crying when she gets angry.

Mickey describes her mind as a logical one but admits to not being very disciplined. Others have detected ice water in her veins, but she shrugs that notion off, although she is known for keeping her head and cool. She has a mathematician's ability to focus—to "find meat" in some event or piece of information.

---

She has a mathematician's ability to focus—to "find meat" in some event or piece of information.

---

She stays extremely fit. No coffee is in the house and dinner is her only meal of the day. She plays golf and has a treadmill and Exercycle in the next room but admits she needs to do more than step around the equipment.

What her trading experience has taught Mickey is that she can be independent and hold her own in any group. After all, she was the first. Along the way, she didn't find it necessary to shed her femininity to work alongside "the boys" in the pit or compete against them on the racquetball court. Although she enjoys to be in control, she has learned when to back off. She has a great sense of humor and enjoys a good joke. Mickey recalls the camaraderie: "It was one big cocktail party." She is still "buddies" with many of her male colleagues.

A best trading moment and best opportunity for learning was her last trade. Mickey has not had a worst trading moment yet. There isn't anything she feels she can't handle. When I asked if she had ever felt intimidated, she answered firmly, "No, only on the tennis court!"

She believes you make your successes. This definitely does not mean judging success in terms of money. Although money is how the score is kept, she describes success as a complete package of inner self-contentment. On the other hand, "you have to be hungry" to go after something. If things could be going better, you "smile bigger."

Mickey remembered being teased by some of the guys on the floor about having nothing to show for her trading success. Just this one time she went out with them and bought a Mercedes on the spot. It was blue. She never had to do that again.

She lives well but is hardly extravagant. She is generous with her support of philanthropic activities, especially those involving children and sports. "I believe sports is a great training ground and a great deal of what a game requires is also useful in the marketplace." It's a positive way to channel aggression. It teaches patience, persistence, and timing, all of which certainly come into play in trading. In her trading career, Mickey has always kept in mind the big picture and has hung on to a position if she felt it was correct, no matter what anyone else did.

Mickey's advice to someone, especially a woman, contemplating a career in commodities trading is an unqualified "do it." It develops and engages the mind in a daily scene that in many ways bristles with the energy and excitement of a championship sports game. She is totally convinced it's a wonderful field to be in. A good day is enormously satisfying. There's the awareness of interconnection in the world and that you are part of the stream. "You get to associate with a lot of unforgettable people."

It's been a great way to make a living. It's been fun. It's a high-stakes game that she learned to play extremely well. Although Mickey has relied on her own skills, she has a lucky rabbit's foot and has worn hockey pins on her jacket lapel. She would do it over in a minute—but start younger! "It's been a very good life."

# Wild Ride

## CAROL HANCOCK

Trading is the kind of business that produces legends. As the first woman member to trade at the Chicago Board of Trade (CBOT), Carol Ovitz Hancock is a legend. A pioneer on notoriously tough terrain, she faced many of the hardships that come with trailblazing.

I met Carol at the die-casting company she and her husband own and operate. She has been actively involved with the business on a daily basis since leaving trading. We had talked by phone and I was warmly greeted by an attractive low-key woman who spoke in modulated tones, hardly the kind of person who shattered barriers and in effect scaled the ramparts of the Board of Trade and broke through the traditional networks that had always held fast against any female members. The exceptions were the absentee holders of memberships that were merely pieces of real estate, enabling members to pay lower commissions on trades. Women had a muted presence as support staff in secretarial and clerical positions. As far as trading was concerned, the message was clear: "No Women Need Apply." Carol Hancock was to change a 121-year-old policy. Not by resorting to litigation or relying on alliances with various support groups but simply by her refusal to accept the status quo and by proving herself.

---

Carol Hancock was to change a 121-year-old policy.

Not by resorting to litigation or relying on alliances

with various support groups but simply by her refusal

to accept the status quo and by proving herself.

---

Carol grew up in the small Illinois town of Sycamore with a population of about 7,000. She was the oldest of five children, and her mother died when she was quite young. Summer work experience early on included detasseling corn on hot summer days relieved by water fights. She also did a stint in an ice cream store. She recalls it as "all very serendipitous." Through her physician father, who knew someone, she had some summertime experience filling in at a brokerage firm during her years at Smith College. She was filing annual reports when someone in the commodities department got sick, and Carol was called on to man the phones. It went a lot faster than filing. The next summer she was back.

After graduating from Smith with a degree in psychology, she took a year off and traveled around Europe. She admits to not having given much thought to what she would do after "broadening herself."

Rather than go to graduate school, Carol worked in the time-honored position of apprentice handling a trading firm's smaller customers, learning as much as she could on the phone. She also learned a great deal from a man she worked with who traded several major commercial accounts. Carol viewed this as a valuable and necessary apprenticeship, especially when there was a wave of orders.

In 1969, she bought a seat for $20,000 on the CBOT because she "wanted to be part of the industry I felt was about to enter a major period of growth and expansion." In addition to having a seat, another requirement for CBOT membership, according to the bylaws, was being over 21 and male. Carol met the age stipulation. The "male" part wasn't so easy. I've included copies of two letters that are indeed historical documents. The first is one Carol composed and submitted to the CBOT's membership. The second is the very welcoming and positive reply by the chairman of the CBOT.

Carol was the only one who thought she was eligible to trade. Her claim of eligibility was considered a joke. Women weren't even allowed on the floor as visitors! There had been women runners but only to make up for wartime manpower shortages. Carol put up with a lot of not very friendly nudging. "One woman who came later wore construction boots to protect her feet in the pit!" Carol was told her first day on the floor that she had another thing coming if she thought she was going into the pit.

Carol got her first big break when the CBOT decided to use her to publicize a new trade, the iced broiler. I suppose the prevailing thinking at the time was that real men traded grains. Let the little woman have some chicken. That was all she needed. Once someone showed her what to do with her hands, there was no turning her back.

After that she traded wheat as a position trader and earned the respect of her fellow traders. "I saw myself as being in the business of thinking." At the time, position traders had superior access to information to support their trading decisions.

———————————————

"I saw myself as being in the business of thinking."

———————

May 21, 1969


Mr. William J. Mallers
Chairman of the Board
Board of Trade of the City of Chicago
141 West Jackson Boulevard
Chicago, Illinois 60604


Dear Mr. Mallers:

As you are aware, I have been desirous of joining the Chicago Board of Trade for a very considerable period of time. My reasons are quite simple:

1.  I feel your investigation will show that I am properly qualified.
2.  I work with large clients whose activities contribute significantly to your volume, and I feel such a recognition would enable me to be more effective.
3.  I feel women are an increasingly important part of the financial community.
4.  I believe our contribution to your organization will increase.

I do not intend to create any problem or embarrassment to the Chicago Board of Trade, but I do wish to solidfy my intent by filing an application for membership. Such an application may be held in abeyance by yourselves until such a time as you deem proper.

I have asked Mr. Edwin L. Cox of Dallas and Mr. Owen Nichols of Chicago to act as my sponsors; both gentlement have agreed. All three of us wish to conduct the handling of my application in a manner consistent with our business ideals and befitting the standards of the Board of Trade.

My absolute and only intent is to further my own career and to be a part of your organization in its future, which I believe to be dynamic.

Sincerely,

*Carol J. Ovitz*

Carol J. Ovitz

# BOARD OF TRADE
## OF THE CITY OF CHICAGO

HENRY H. WILSON
PRESIDENT

December 22, 1969

Dear Carol:

Little did we know last summer, when you "made history," that so much pleasure would come from setting aside 121 years of tradition at the Chicago Board of Trade.

Perhaps the attached book will serve as a token of our appreciation for the charming, thoughtful, and cooperative way in which you have served the Board and your fellow members during the past six months. In it, you will find some representative samples of the coverage you have received all over the nation and, we hope, memories you will look upon fondly in years to come.

It is a pleasure to have you as a member.

Warmest best wishes for the holiday season.

Sincerely,

Henry H. Wilson

Henry H. Wilson

. . . and your many friends at
the Chicago Board of Trade.

Miss Carol Ovitz
Chicago Board of Trade
Chicago, Illinois

Carol recalls that the ladies' room was four floors away and that it was many years before a closer one was provided. "When I received my 25-year plaque, it still referred to 'him.'" Carol recalls, "Once I was down there, I was treated as an equal." She had demonstrated her skill and professionalism at what had traditionally been, for all intents and purposes, an exclusive male financial club.

What made her think she could do it? Well, "my senior thesis had been on vision!" Perhaps Carol could see herself in this hostile environment that she put up with to attain her goals. She certainly "saw" things in the markets that others missed. "I enjoyed the intellectual challenge and the excitement." She considered herself in the information business as she built grain or soybean positions based on her thinking about data and news that was available to all.

Going to work, her adrenaline would start pumping in preparation for what she had to face. When she started dating her future husband, Carol was reluctant to talk about the financial risks she faced on a daily basis but finally had to admit to the possibility that she could "lose the farm" on a bad day.

She found it harder to go home and switch to being a mother. Before her daughter was born, she could relax by exercising. It's not easy to change gears after having your mind "fried," even for a psych major.

What helped get her through was that trading never occupied her entire life. "I always had other interests." She is an accomplished photographer who has sold her work. There's also skiing, which is a great mind clearer. She has been able to travel extensively and has visited Africa and Asia. She is also a capable crew member and serves as navigator on a boat she and her husband, a research scientist whom she met on a blind date, take out. When asked to describe her relationship to the market and her role, Carol sees the market as a sea. Her role was to steer, make good corners while taking advantage of the wind, and go the distance. And keep tacking! She also enjoys regular walks with a friend and with her dog, who is also by her side at her present work. This is a high-energy individual who enjoys being fully engaged in a variety of pursuits.

What Carol learned about herself from trading was that she had the discipline required as well as reserves of tenacity when called for. In this business, as in her classes at Smith, she was after an "A." A strong competitive layer lurks beneath her polished surface. One of the most difficult aspects for Carol, or any trader, was picking herself up after a hard day, "licking her wounds," as she put it.

Carol also clearly recalls that it was scary and lonesome in the early days. She was single and put up with being called "doll" by an older position trader. Carol wasn't about to mind as he was going to keep an eye out for her. Position traders tended to look out for each other more than "scalpers" did.

She rose to a challenge she gave herself. "It was a matter of catching a ball that was thrown to me." It was an opportunity she had to go after. Her trading rule was simple: "I'm going to be here tomorrow!" Also, she was "not interested in converting small pickles into major ones."

Along the way Carol learned how to temper the effects of extremes. The learning curve was supported by the solid masonry of experience. She credits her sailing experience with contributing to her ability to use her instinct as a guide.

Unavoidable were the painful down episodes. "The only way to get through them was to pretend to be someone else." At such times, going out with a camera helped change her focus.

The best way to deal with the ever present possibility of loss was by managing the risk, keeping her mental frame of mind clear, and never "trading scared." Although she is strong-willed, Carol is in agreement with the other women described in this book that a big ego is a male thing.

Success to her resided in having clearly thought out what the market would do, assuming a position based on this, and getting it right. She went to great lengths, however, to leave her thoughts at work so she could get a good night's sleep.

To get along with the variety of humanity found on the trading floor, and especially in the centrifuge of the pit, "it was essential to be completely comfortable with myself." It was "kind of rough" but she does miss the jokes. No matter what the situation, a joke would emerge from it and serve as a mini stress reducer.

Carol took full advantage of the intellectual challenge trading presented. "I went there to learn and sometimes felt like a bystander at the edge of a football game in full turmoil." She is convinced that no one can stop someone who is completely interested in learning and participating. "I also enjoyed the crazy aspects of trading and the colorful cast of characters."

She remembers "many times leaving for the day thinking I'd been quite brilliant, only to have all my assumptions questioned by the following day's market turn." There were times when she felt intimidated by events and wondered how she could have been so stupid as to have managed to miss a particular opportunity.

On Black Tuesday in 1987, Carol came home with a fearful noise in her head telling her that what was happening was a force greater than herself. There was no way to control it. It didn't affect her. Her grain spreads rode out the storm.

---

On Black Tuesday in 1987, Carol came home with a fearful noise in her head telling her that what was happening was a force greater than herself. There was no way to control it.

---

She always looked for opportunities in the market and for the most part found them—curious bits of news revealing shortages and surpluses that would influence supply and demand and play out in interesting ways.

In her "mature years," she tried to learn the lesson of "hubris": Bulls make money, bears make money, but greedy pigs get slaughtered." She would build a position in small increments, nursing it along until the right moment arrived to shave off half, keeping in mind that "you never go broke taking a profit."

Carol enjoyed the adrenaline rush at the time but feels her brand of trading had its golden age and involves too much risk in the markets' current financial climate.

Although not eager to have her college-age daughter follow in her footsteps, Carol encourages anyone who senses it's for them to go and try this "hard way to make an easy living." The tricky part is finding the opportunity to learn. Carol has carried over her skills to her position as executive vice president of her die-casting business. She continues to persevere in improving the business and increasing its profits. She is certainly subject to less stress and welcomes taking three-day weekends when she and her husband can simply sail away with dog on deck. Yes, she would do it all again!

# Family Business

Leslie Henner Burns's name kept popping up from several people who knew of my project. Our children also attended the same school. My first call found her nursing a sick child. The next time everyone was off to Disney World. When I arrived for our appointment at her relaxing home overseen by her husband, a former trader who has a possibly more relentless role as stay-at-home dad, Leslie was just arriving, only slightly preceding her children.

A dark-haired woman with an open, interested face, she reminded me of a high-level professional such as a pediatrician, lawyer, or psychiatrist. Here she was with the day's pit dust still clinging to her, and she was ready to devote the time to tell her story.

As a third-generation trader, Leslie is carrying on the "family business." Her grandfather was a legendary "omelet maker" in the old butter-and-egg exchange. Her father followed in his footsteps as has her brother. Having spent 20 years at the Chicago Mercantile Exchange (Merc) after starting out in the T-bill pit before settling down in eurodollars, where she is a major market maker, Leslie had much to say. She grew up in an affluent suburb north of Chicago and had worked as a camp counselor. After graduating from high school, she went to Stanford University, where she earned a B.A. degree in history.

After college Leslie worked for her dad charting markets and "crunching" the numbers. It's usually not easy working for a family member, particularly your father. He simply told her to let him know if she saw anything interesting. That was all she had to hear to produce a steady stream of "tradeworthy" information. She seemed to be taking to the family business. "I had always believed that there was nothing I couldn't accomplish if I set my mind to it." At the end of the summer after college graduation, when she was 21, Leslie became a member of the Merc. It was the first family transfer on that exchange.

Her father encouraged her to try out her ideas in the pit where she would get immediate feedback and could find out if she was right or wrong. This instant replay appealed to her and she kept at it, learning as much as she could, especially when she was wrong. She collected an impressive number of winners by scalping the markets.

After hearing her dad say that women couldn't fill orders, Leslie proved him wrong by becoming an order filler any dad would be proud of.

She went on to trade Treasury bills for five years until the contract dried up and she moved on to the greener pastures of the pit for the newly created eurodollar, where she developed into one of its biggest players.

Reflecting on her early work experience, she remembers, "It was awful!" The markets were capricious and required tremendous tenacity and agility. Although her dad was her mentor, "nobody ever shared trading secrets with me. The attitude was that all traders paid for their own education." Leslie remembers thinking, "I was always in danger of making the same mistake in different guises." When I heard this, I thought of the popular children's book, *Where's Waldo?*, where the character Waldo must be found in ever-different crowds and scenes.

---

The markets were capricious and required

tremendous tenacity and agility. Although her dad

was her mentor, "nobody ever shared trading secrets

with me. The attitude was that all traders paid for

their own education."

---

A quiet woman, Leslie admits she makes herself heard. Intellectually, she is adept at combining many diverse elements. A lifelong perfectionist, Leslie found herself always seeking that elusive creature, the perfect trade. Does it even exist?

She feels she has grown on the job and has a "civilizing effect" on her rowdy, unruly fellow traders. She has a definite code of behavior and refuses to use the rampant foul language of what she considers a locker-room atmosphere. "I always strive to be cool, calm, and reasonable," good qualities that work in any environment. She tries to avoid outright anger because she considers the consequence too expensive. "It's essential to choose one's battles with great care." As a big trader, she gets respect that she draws on for maximum benefit. Leslie has far exceeded her original goal of just showing her dad and herself that she could do it.

She has steadily progressed from lower lows and lower highs to higher lows and higher highs. Leslie is convinced that "the difficult path ultimately leads to better and higher ground." Her complex, highly organized trading style would challenge the busiest air traffic controller. She feels she has gained a lot of strength and self-knowledge, which has really bolstered her self-esteem.

Her workday goes from 7:20 in the morning until 4:00 in the afternoon. Often Leslie's work follows her home as she keeps current with worldwide markets. She wakes up ready to go. After a bowl of

Grape-Nuts and a cup of tea (like several other women in this book, she has given up coffee), her husband drives her to work so they can spend some time together.

Although she does her best to separate her work from the rest of her life, she does find herself taking it home. "I have even dreamed about relationships in the market!" Leslie relaxes by reading to herself and her children. A quietly vibrant woman, she has also started skiing in addition to having a long list of interests that includes travel, tennis, snorkeling, golf, board games, and puzzles. She is not one to sit around doing nothing.

Leslie believes that her focus, tenacity, skill with numbers, historical perspective, and ability to connect events, as well as her interest in games, have all contributed to her trading talent. Over the years she has developed a certain feel for the market and an ability "to listen" to its voice. As she says, it's "an inner thing."

Leslie also believes a sense of humor is a vital survival skill. She remembers the joking around in the pit, which not only serves as a valuable pressure valve but provides perspective.

Trading has taught her to fine-tune her ability to focus. All of her life she has had a drive to be good at whatever she did, whether trading eurodollars or baking bread! She views her work as a compelling as well as consuming part of her makeup. She is the breadwinner of her family and it's very good bread!

---

"It's a battle of wits in which, depending on the strategies, everybody can succeed and make money." No one has to go hungry unless he or she hasn't played well.

Leslie views trading as a rigorous intellectual exercise with major consequences for both sides. "It's a battle of wits in which, depending on the strategies, everybody can succeed and make money." No one has to go hungry unless he or she hasn't played well."

She enjoys her exciting work. "Most of the time. I couldn't think of another occupation I would find as satisfying. I am totally bonded with this one." Leslie advises any woman starting out to be really strong. What she is referring to is inner strength. A deep understanding of oneself is absolutely essential. In addition, you have to pay your dues. Do your homework—in other words, pony up for your education just as she did.

Leslie feels she has developed a necessary toughness. Knowing what she does about the difficulties involved in trading, she would still want her children to do it!

Leslie has a few lucky charms. Pinned to the lapel of her trading jacket is an "S" for Stanford next to the teddy bear her children gave her. In her pocket there is always a tiny, old, much folded, and dog-eared piece of paper. It has only one word on it: "Fool." This was a message from her dad many years ago when she knew a lot less than she does now.

Would she do it all over again? Leslie is relieved that she doesn't have to start over but, without a moment's hesitation, lets me know the answer is "absolutely, without any question!"

# CHAPTER 5

# Broker-Mom

## KAREN DOHERTY

It took several calls to hook up with Karen Doherty, a single mom with two teenagers who lives on Chicago's South Side. When we finally talked, the connection was bad because one of the kids had dropped the phone in the toilet. Two days later, on a sunny fall afternoon, I pulled up to the only house in the neighborhood seriously ready for Halloween. Not only was it displaying decorations, the surrounding yard was bursting with impatiens. A basketball hoop was in the back.

My visit turned out to be a surprise because Karen hadn't checked her messages. She had taken a rare day off from work to do some gardening. Sipping ice tea and listening to her children as they came home with greetings and friends, we sat outside on the terrace of her simple but comfortable—and very homey and cheery—house.

I liked Karen immediately. She's friendly, open, Irish, down-to-earth. This was going to be good. What was her path to the Chicago Board of Trade, where she's spent 18 years, the last 15 as a broker? I feel she belongs in this book because she deals with many of the same issues as the other women here and has succeeded in a sea of men.

Karen comes from a working-class background. Her dad was a clerical worker for the city who tended bar at night to make ends meet. Her mom was a housewife. Karen has a twin sister and five brothers, two of whom trade. There is also her brother, Frank, a bond trader who has played an important role in her career.

She grew up poor in the material sense but has nothing but good things to say about her family. As a child she missed a lot of school because of severe asthma. Karen didn't let this difficulty prevent her from keeping her mind active by playing cards with her mom and working on puzzles. She felt these were valuable experiences that even now help her keep her cards in order.

It was not expected that she go to college but that she get married and then pregnant. "I wasn't going to do that." She was really ahead of her time. After studying sociology in a small college in California, she worked in a Dean Witter back office as operations manager. She also toyed with the idea of opening up a plant shop where she could put her gardening skills to work. Karen took advantage of a three-year permit program the firm offered, and her brother Frank loaned her money to buy a seat. If he believed in her capacity to meet the challenge, she could believe in herself. She was on her way, and it wasn't long before she paid him back.

Karen recalled her first day of trading, when she looked around her and remembered thinking, "This is nuts. I'll never be able to do it." Later that day, "I sat on my sister's steps and cried, but I was back in the pits the next day!" Karen remembered being told by a veteran trader to think of trading as a new language. That was useful advice that helped her to learn what was going on and to participate in the wild conversation that roared around her.

Karen recalled her first day of trading, when she looked around her and remembered thinking, "This is nuts. I'll never be able to do it." Later that day, "I sat on my sister's steps and cried, but I was back in the pits the next day!"

She started out trading Ginnie Maes, a very busy contract, and now handles options on ten-year Treasury notes. She works with five guys, rents out her CBOT seat, and uses her options seat. In her words, "This is where the party is!" She is fervently independent and believes that working hard pays off.

Karen had always worked at a variety of jobs, everything from assisting in a stamp collecting business, selling magazines, and waitressing at a hamburger joint to working as a cocktail waitress. Her exposure to a wide range of personalities and her ability to adapt to new situations helped her meet the challenges of her new environment.

Karen feels fortunate that two of her brothers, including Frank, who had helped his siblings get started—were already on the floor. The brothers were well known by the time Karen arrived on the scene and looked out for her. She also learned her "market smarts" from them. The CBOT has a reputation for being "Appalachian" in the sense that everybody seems to be related. Family members take care of their own.

At this point in her life, Karen feels there is no day she can't get through. She works from seven in the morning until two in the afternoon and likes to be home to greet her children when they arrive from school. She is also lucky to have a housekeeper who is like a member of the family. During the day she takes an hour off to clear her head. Her advice about dealing with the pressure is "don't bring it home." She relaxes by walking, biking, and gardening. She enjoys reading.

Being a single parent keeps Karen busy. Taking time to talk with her kids is high on her list. They also go skiing in Colorado and rent a beach house in California. Her hard work has enabled her to give her family options she didn't have as a child. Her close-knit family gathers for reunions in Florida as often as they can all get together. She has traveled to Ireland and was anticipating a first trip to Paris with her daughter and her twin, whose daughter is studying there.

Karen has maintained her balance in a high-octane setting by sheer determination. "I'm good with numbers and quick on my feet." Speaking of feet, she is of average height and likes to stand on a top step in the pit. Above all, she doesn't get flustered and advises those contemplating this career choice to keep their cool. Whatever happens, Karen just handles it. During downtime, she can let her mind wander even when she can't, and there's time for talking and joking around. She considers herself a member of the group but on her terms.

---

Karen has maintained her balance in a high-octane setting by sheer determination. "I'm good with numbers and quick on my feet."

---

Karen believes in diplomacy rather than armed combat. People who work in close quarters with each other on a daily basis can't let things build. It might get in the way of work that is hard enough as it is. She sees herself as a professional who can follow through and not give until the job's done.

Her experience on the floor has taught her that she is effective and can do the job. This has been very strengthening. "I'm competitive and have no problem taking what I consider my fair share." Even though she grew up in a traditional Irish South Side setting, nobody ever told her she couldn't do something. "Having those brothers didn't hurt!"

If Karen has any rules that she uses on the floor, they are keeping cool and trying to be as fair as possible.

She can't recall the last time she felt intimidated. Whatever happens, "it's important to not turn it into an issue." Karen advises: Act like you know what you're doing, understand the fundamentals, keep it light. And take classes to keep up with a constantly and rapidly changing industry.

What she has really enjoyed over the years are the friendships she's developed with her colleagues, male and female. Karen met her former husband, who was her best customer, on the floor.

She compared the floor to a locker room or a frat party. She feels like she sees *Animal House* on a daily basis.

She worries about burning out, a very real phenomenon not unlike battle fatigue that does afflict active veterans on the floor. In the future, Karen sees herself doing something more altruistic, although she doesn't yet know what. The majority of women in the industry that I talked with believe in, and do, "give back" in a variety of ways that range from charity to helping family members. One woman supported an entire family in Sri Lanka. Other occupations that Karen would consider and find fulfilling include the garden/ gift shop she had considered after college, social work, or speech pathology.

Karen is close to the brother who is still on the floor. She has noticed with regret a growing lack of camaraderie in the pit and remarked on the increase in "road rage" that she has experienced firsthand. To avoid it, she usually takes the train to work. The ride helps her relax and prepare for the active day of "filling 'em and billing 'em" and "banging them out quick" that awaits her. She's not superstitious but prefers not to see black cats and keeps walking under ladders to a minimum.

---

She's not superstitious but prefers not to see black cats and keeps walking under ladders to a minimum.

---

Karen tries to keep everything in perspective. She also feels that money is the ultimate god for far too many. "A good day is one when I'm fairly active." She doesn't take the work problems home and looks forward to spending time with her family. "In many ways," she adds, "my day really starts when I can spend time with my family." She likes to make dinner and attend her children's soccer, basketball, baseball, and volleyball games. She also likes to play golf.

During the course of the interview I met Karen's twin sister, an elementary school teacher whose former husband was also in the trading business and had "lost it all." The close relationship with her sister keeps Karen from feeling isolated, especially as a single parent. Karen has drawn strength throughout her life from this bond as well as from the rest of her large and caring family. I also heard so much about the other members of her family that I felt as if I had met them all in person.

One very important role model in Karen's life was her grandfather on her mother's side. She remembers him as a kind and loving man who had always lived with her family. He had great success building theaters, and although he lost everything in the depression, he remained a charming character and lived past the age of 90.

Her advice to anyone starting out would be to believe in yourself—that you can do the job as well as anybody else. She is convinced it's more about temperament and less about mechanics, more about standing your ground. It's a people business and "you've got to enjoy all the Campbell soup varieties."

Karen plans to trade until she finds something else. She has devoted a large part of her life to an extremely demanding profession and feels she has earned the right to, and can afford to, ease up. This doesn't mean retirement, just finding a new challenge.

Trading has been great financially and has afforded her and her children a lifestyle she could only dream about as a child. They have the freedom to select from a wide array of options. She used to identify herself with her work but now perceives it as more of a challenge than the fun it used to be. Karen also feels the physical effects more as she is growing older. "I want to see my children doing something else with their life."

She feels secure in her self-esteem and ability to chart her course in a new direction. Nevertheless, when asked if she would be willing to do it all over again, she replied, "Yeah, I would." It has been fun and exciting but she wouldn't want "the party to last so long."

# CHAPTER 6

# Global Trader

ARLENE BUSCH

Arlene Busch's reputation accompanies her in her travels throughout the worldwide trading circles that are like different areas in her office. Arlene is one of a few women who have made it to the pinnacles of a male-dominated industry. She has tremendous knowledge and skill and is well wired within the industry network. Things happen wherever she is. They usually involve megaincreases in profits. She is truly a phenomenon in her chosen minefield. Nothing less than the hard-to-reach top would have satisfied her in whatever career she selected. Her résumé reads like the financial section of a major newspaper. She has built her dossier by assuming responsibilities in the high-stakes financial nervous system of the international marketplace.

She has recently relocated to New York to head an asset management group valued at $700 million.

I was fortunate enough to have the opportunity to hear her story during a brief visit she made to Chicago, where it all began. The diminutive woman, clad in an impeccable champagne outfit, and I got down to business, which is how she deals with life. The telephone was always by her hand at the ready so she could follow the progress of market plays she had put in place in the daily financial superbowl that the world's markets resemble a competition with an unbelievable number of contenders. While we talked she managed to make a subtantial amount of money.

Everything Arlene's achieved has been the result of her own focused force. She grew up poor in Chicago. Her father had a newsstand and her mother worked as a receptionist. Early on, it was clear to her that whatever she wanted in life she would have to achieve on her own. Planning to teach, she studied chemistry and math at nearby Northeastern Illinois University so she could live at home and save money. A night job as an AT&T information operator paid her way. She has remained a firm believer in the global information flow.

When Arlene was 26, her mother died of cancer. It was an extremely difficult time in her life, although she had already been taking care of herself for some time by "hustling" backgammon and playing bridge. She has always enjoyed and excelled at games. Referring to her professional career, she said, "The marbles had just gotten bigger."

Game by game, she just kept moving ahead toward a better life. Her urge to achieve was in the cards. Arlene admits to being a driven, high-performing type A personality that just doesn't stop until desired goals are reached and, in her case, customarily surpassed. There is always some other financial frontier to be conquered.

Her first taste of trading was at the Chicago Board Options Exchange (CBOE), and she liked it immediately. "I came to trade." Arlene began as a clerk and learned as she went along. "I always tried to stand behind traders who looked like they knew what they were doing." It was only a matter of time before she knew enough to "sit down at the table" or, in this case, to go toe-to-toe with the other traders. She was drawn to the immediate feedback. "You find out right away if you're right or wrong."

Her ability was quickly recognized. Arlene had not one, but three, mentors. She learned something valuable from each one. One was very technical. Another practiced a more speculative seat-of-the-pants approach. When she was ready, all three backed her.

Arlene seems immune to the stress and seeks out risk. She moved on to increasingly challenging responsibilities. There was nothing she couldn't handle. The more she took on, the more knowledge and confidence she gained. "I learned to always have control over any outcome and to never make a career decision I couldn't afford." In her own words, "You always want to be able to show up the next day."

She spent some time at the Chicago Board of Trade during the infancy of a new product—bond options—where she became a market maker in a highly volatile field. Next was relocation to London where Arlene set up a highly lucrative brokerage business. It wasn't exciting enough, and she left to create ever more complex financial networks.

Space doesn't permit me to detail the dense professional trail Arlene has left around the world. This woman is a whirlwind who seeks out risk and is expert at making it work for her. What her professional credentials can teach is that if you want it, you can do it. Every move she made was planned, and every move worked. Her highly competitive nature finds other outlets in racquetball, and she is a bridge master. Arlene considers trading the ultimate game!

When we met, she was taking a rare opportunity (I won't call it rest) to assess her impressive options and reach for the next rung. I would think rest would not be relaxing for someone with this high energy. As we talked, an image of metal came to mind. I thought of titanium. Light and strong.

Stress and risk don't seem to affect Arlene, but she still enjoys tennis, running, walking, and aerobic exercise as well as reading. On really bad days, she used to go home, curl up in a ball, and go the sleep. To give an idea of her scale, she has had million-dollar losing days but never a losing month! That's a long way from "hustling" backgammon.

Her professional life has taken a toll on her personal one, but this has been a choice she has made and expected. She's been married twice, but domestic family life is simply not in the picture. She prefers moving around the world's financial hot spots. She has succeeded spectacularly in a male-dominated field, which has to be threatening to many men. Her success might also be a point of vulnerability under certain circumstances. Arlene has been willing to pay the price to do what a lot of people couldn't handle.

---

Her professional life has taken a toll on her personal

one, but this has been a choice she has made

and expected.

---

Arlene does admit to being treated differently because she is a woman, but she has used this to her advantage in an industry that is still notoriously difficult for women, particularly those at the higher levels. She is only slightly intimidated by a male who is faster than she is. "I handle it by respecting his talent and getting on with the business at hand." She has tremendous discipline, which enables her to succeed in the perilous financial waters she finds so stimulating. Her work is what really makes her feel alive. To extend a time-honored analogy, "A good day is better than sex!" The only other role she can see herself in is that of a trial lawyer.

As for a trading rule, "Take each day as it comes." She knows that no matter what she has planned, the market is always right and deserves respect. "I try to take nothing, including myself, for granted." One of her life rules is to find something to appreciate each day. She tries to separate work from nonwork.

Money is the scorecard, but Arlene measures her professional success by the respect she has earned from her peers and by her secure position in her field. "I believe in fair dealing, in knowing what you're doing, in doing what you say you'll do, and in delivering on promises. Only then is it reasonable to expect the same in return." It is important for her to be able to look in the mirror and like what she sees.

---

"I believe in fair dealing, in knowing what you're

doing, in doing what you say you'll do, and in

delivering on promises. Only then is it reasonable to

expect the same in return."

---

She advises anyone starting out to learn on someone else's money, to pick a good mentor, and to keep in mind that if you are passionate about your work, it should make you happy and fulfilled.

Her experience is her lucky charm. In addition, she supports a family in Sri Lanka and hopes they say an occasional prayer for her.

Arlene thoroughly enjoys her work and considers it fun. She appreciates the fact that it is always different. "I've been very lucky." If she had to do it all over again, "I would do it exactly the same." She who expects, accepts, and knows how to manage risk is never disappointed.

# CHAPTER 7

# Oh No

## MARY MacDIARMID

It was a Sunday morning in the fall. Leaves were sticking to the sidewalk on a quiet Chicago street. The sky looked like a soft old gray sweatshirt. I climbed to the third floor and pushed the buzzer. There was a little heart-shaped wreath on the door.

Mary MacDiarmid looked more like a college senior or grad student than the seasoned trader I knew she was. She is tall—six feet—and was comfortably dressed in leggings, socks, and an old shirt. She tried to restrain a golden Labrador she was taking care of for a friend. Her apartment was cozy and adorned with many twiggy hearts, gifts from her mother who knew she liked them. There were also fine Chinese antiques and a collection of elephants in differing shapes and sizes.

A Carole King record was playing in the background. There was a feeling of peace and spirituality. We went into the kitchen and sat down at a table in front of a window. Mary lit a candle. The dog settled down at her feet and we began. She has been trading eurodollar options for seven years. It all began when she answered a classified ad for a "trader's assistant." For all she knew she might end up as a wizard's apprentice! She was to be a clerk. As a math major, numbers were second nature to her and she was drawn to the quickness. Two days after being hired, she was told she would be trading.

She liked the idea of trading in theory. It was fast like skiing down the expert run. In practice she found it difficult and scary. She reminded herself of the saying by Albert Camus, "That which does not kill you makes you stronger." Basically, she was just thrown in like an unprepared puppy flung into a ring of pit bulls. "I thought it was absolutely nuts and asked myself what I was doing there!" Her trading symbol reads "Oh No" and eloquently represents her initial response. As an experienced trader, Mary knows there is always the possibility of an "oh no" situation. She also knows that she has to be prepared to anticipate those times or, when it's too late, to deal with it.

Mary didn't know if she could do it but she did know that she wanted to. It was a challenge. "I will always pick up a gauntlet that someone has thrown down."

————————————

Mary didn't know if she could do it but she did know

that she wanted to. It was a challenge. "I will always

pick up a gauntlet that someone has thrown down."

————

She has always taken the steeper path and likes rising to the challenge. Even when she is driving, Mary likes to calculate her average speed. She needs to supply her active mind with something to do. Although she admits to being a poor speller, she loves to read a wide variety of material. She also enjoys cooking.

Mary grew up as the middle of three sisters in an affluent Chicago suburb. Her parents work together at their real estate development business. "My family is the rock I lean on." She hasn't needed a safety net, but it's comforting to know it's there. Mary credits her family and the upbringing it provided as the source of her strength. According to her parents, there was nothing she couldn't do or succeed in.

She did okay in high school but was considered a bright underachiever who didn't apply herself until a physics teacher threw down the gauntlet and Mary rose to the occasion.

She went on to attend a small Catholic girl's college, St. Mary's, where she was fortunate enough to pick up another gauntlet. This one was dropped by a math professor, a nun with a Ph.D. from the University of Chicago who had taught three generations of students.

Mary's prior work experience had been in retail and at a community swimming pool, which was similar in its frenzied activity to the trading pit she was to inhabit later. She also worked at a law firm and considered going on to law school.

There are many people with similar backgrounds who don't end up as successful young traders. Mary found out that trading suited her personality. The pit was filled with gauntlets flying and trampled underfoot that were thrown by the market and its participants.

The challenge of trading was unlike anything Mary had faced before. She learned mainly by trial and error. "My senior thesis in college on multiple linear regression proved a help because almost all pricing is based on regression analysis." Also present was the speed of the action. Mary says that it's all in her head. "I'm not a sheet monkey," as she expresses it.

She seems to get a real adrenaline rush from thinking through a problem the way an athlete gets a similar sensation from a physical feat.

Her mind needs to play as well as work. Mary enjoys playing Jeopardy and her concentrated involvement in a game of Tetris once caused her to miss a flight. She takes thinking very seriously and finds it entertaining to devise mental scenarios that usually involve numbers and information.

When Mary started trading in December 1991, she was the only one to get "badged up" in her office, the local expression for receiving a trading badge. "I remember thinking that I was not in the frying pan but in the fire!" No question but what it had to be tried. She was pretty much on her own as she had a mainly absentee boss who would check on how things were going and growing.

The boss was a good mentor by allowing Mary to fall on her face and pick herself up again. He wasn't breathing down her neck, although she does recall one time when he publicly called her out of the pit like a coach benching a player. Overall he had confidence in her demonstrated ability to conduct his business. She recalls, "Even when he was wrong he was right!" He was certainly right in his judgment about her.

Mary prepares herself physically by doing cardiorespiratory exercises, playing volleyball or tennis, and running. Mentally, she is ready to go, to enter "the zone." Mary finds out what the opening call is and moves on to make markets.

On bad days, "I take time out to think through my mistakes and try to learn from them and then reenter slowly." If she's not trading effectively, she tries to figure out what to do rather than "beating herself up." She tries to accept her limitations; she'll say, for example, "I'm not the only person who can do it. Others deserve a chance to play." When she was first starting out, Mary tended to let her trading control her. She carried a beeper around and even dreamed about trading. Now she feels she's more in control. She sometimes can't leave her work "at the office," but she has learned not to obsess about it. "It's no longer a big deal."

Mary's stature is definitely an asset, and she has had voice training more for protecting her voice than anything else. She sang in high school and knows it's necessary to reach the audience. She also feels her seeming immunity to offensive behavior is a definite advantage. She is never at a loss for words. I can see her easily portraying one of Shakespeare's strong, memorable women who talk their way eloquently through problems.

As far as Mary's concerned, "Everyone is fair game." It's an equal playing field and the ability to poke fun at yourself helps fill those lulls in the field.

Another helpful quality is her relatively thick skin. Her experiences with crude friends have served to prepare her for pit etiquette and its absence. Mary is not easily intimidated, having learned to deal with intimidation in her rookie trading days. She prides herself on giving as good, if not better, than she gets. Many times, the most effective response is to ignore threatening behavior. Mary enjoys the jokes for which the pits have a well-deserved reputation for producing and marketing.

The banter of the pits is a means of relating and of posturing as well as of reducing tension. Mary is very quick-witted. "I do have a deserved reputation for my sharp tongue!" For the future she sees herself as married with children or as "Crazy Old Aunt Mary," an image that causes her more amusement than anxiety. Mary is clearly very independent, choosing to be neither one of the boys nor one of the girls.

---

The banter of the pits is a means of relating and of posturing as well as of reducing tension. Mary is very quick witted. "I do have a deserved reputation for my sharp tongue!"

---

It is crucial in trading to work on maintaining perspective and leaving the atmosphere behind as thoroughly as possible. Mary does volunteer work for a charity begun by a fellow trader: teaching homeless women computer programming so they will have marketable skills.

A former debutante, she also donates her time to charity work sponsored by the Junior League. This social display was something she did to make her parents happy, but she admits it was fun. Mary prefers adult gauntlets to kid gloves!

Trading has provided a necessary and unavoidably humbling experience. "I have always found it very difficult to be wrong. I love to be right. It's the best! It's the best! It's the best!" In other words, being right is very important to her. She has accepted the inevitability of those times when she will be wrong. She has learned that there *is* life after being wrong. You take responsibility, learn from the event, and proceed. No need to wallow; the sooner you take steps, the better. Naturally, she still prefers to be right but has learned to handle the "w" word.

It is essential for Mary to feel good about herself. "Ultimately, I have to answer to myself." She admits she is capable of serious sarcasm that stops short, however, of malice. She would be a most valuable player on a debate team. She enjoys a good verbal duel and is always ready to participate in a stimulating pickup game of words. Guess who usually has the last word!

Mary does not see herself as a "bottom feeder," making money from other people's mistakes. She feels she possesses and practices high standards and adds, "I'm very hard on myself." She is constantly vigilant about greed. Mary is also aware of the danger of self-absorption, feeling you are in your own little world disconnected from the rest of life. In her view it is absolutely critical to maintain that bond, that life support, with regular life.

It might be that she is hard on herself because she feels that God is watching. She is also convinced that "what goes around comes around." A slightly decomposing sheet of paper is taped up on a kitchen cabinet she sees every morning. Its message says quite a lot about Mary's views:

### "Myself" by Edgar Albert Guest

I have to live with myself and so I want to be fit for myself to know.

I want to be able, as the days go by, always to look myself straight in the eye.

I don't want to stand with the setting sun and hate myself for the things I've done.

I don't want to keep on a closet shelf a lot of secrets about myself and fool myself as I come and go into thinking that nobody else will know the kind of (man) I really am.

I don't want to dress myself up in sham.

I want to go out with my head erect and I want to deserve all men's respect but here in the struggle for fame and pelf I want to be able to like myself.

I don't want to think as I come and go that I'm bluster and bluff and empty show.

I never can hide myself from me.

I see what others may never see.

I know what others may never know.

I never can fool myself and so whatever happens I want to be self-respecting and conscience free.

A memorable time came when Mary felt she could trade on her own. She had gained confidence in her ability and could trade independently. "I am very independent." This basic quality is fundamental to her character, and everything she does serves to strengthen this structural beam of her personality.

The question about her worst trading moments produced the response, "Where do we begin?" The first few years were unbelievably tough. Her dad, who knew he had a strong daughter, urged Mary to take time off and go to Colorado. He'd support her while she cleared her head and set her course in a new direction if necessary. It was hard for him to see her struggle and suffer. It's hardly surprising that she chose to stick it out. "I remember working harder. And then just working still harder! Afterwards, there was even harder work." Mary was convinced that trading was not an insoluble problem. She would ultimately figure it out.

Mary has developed a commonsense response to inevitable loss or its extended form, the losing streak. She views her market performance as a report card. She has to work extremely hard for those top grades. This self-induced pressure is balanced by the realization that she is only human. When the market moves in a way she didn't count on, it's a reminder for her to never take anything, including herself, for granted. "Next time, I'll be better prepared. It's always wise to look at a position in its worst-case possibility where I can get killed." She'll study and analyze the reports to see if she's missing something. There is no resting on laurels. Anything more than a slight pause is valuable time lost and the result can be disastrous. This is not a business that attracts couch potatoes!

"A good day is one on which I have made good markets," when the whole operation is running smoothly, she has served the function of a local market maker, and all are playing their respective roles.

Mary likes to think she gets along with her fellow traders, but she prefers a professional distance: "I don't have to like them and I don't have to hate them." She thinks they probably view her as somewhat strange but that doesn't bother her. It gives her a bit of an edge. Another eurodollar options trader who has seen her in action says Mary is one trader who really knows what she's doing. Mary is very selective about who she spends her time with. In between the bursts of activity there's time for some joking around to reduce the stress. When she describes her colleagues as "funny," it's a compliment.

She remains one of a handful of woman in the eurodollar options pit. As far as social life is concerned, she prefers relating to traders. Mary feels "civilians" are incapable of understanding the toll her work takes. At one time she could touch, call to, and wave to her last three boyfriends on the trading floor.

She has a deep need to be by herself to restore herself and return to clear thinking. Mary would like to have more peace in her life, seeking out activities that are "mind sweepers." She likes to let her mind run full throttle to get a good workout. Books on a great variety of subjects were scattered around, obviously read or waiting to be opened.

---

She has a deep need to be by herself to restore

herself and return to clear thinking.

---

Whenever possible, she is always ready to leave the armchair to travel. Mary has explored Europe by Eurorail and visited Iceland as well as the Bahamas. She also enjoys spending downtime in Florida and Colorado. When we spoke, she was anticipating a family Thanksgiving in San Francisco.

Mary normally takes the el to work and finds the trip relaxing. Occasionally, she treats herself to a cab. Her background expresses itself in her lifestyle. "I like to live well but I am on the thrifty side." Mary is definitely the sort of person who will keep a shirt past its prime. She is not a slave to fashion but was anticipating getting dressed for a black-tie political fundraiser that she was involved in. Model tall, blond, natural, all-American; it was apparent she would clean up nicely.

It should not be surprising that Mary likes to be in control. She likes to be behind the wheel on a boat and won't ride unless she's steering. Is it surprising that she has chosen trading as her field? Trading presents an opportunity to exert control in a vast field resembling a daily avalanche of information and financial energy.

World finance takes on a life of its own. There are people all over the globe who think they know which finger of this Gulliver-like market is going to twitch. Everyone is trying to peek behind the screen to see if it's really the formidable Great Oz or a humbug.

I see Mary in the mold of Dorothy from Kansas. Whatever is thrown at her—flying monkeys, witches good or bad—she is going to be able to deal with it until she returns home. She consumes challenges like others go through a bag of potato chips. Mary likes testing herself, passing with flying colors, and moving on to the next flag.

Mary admits to being very competitive at her work but considers it a survival skill. "I see trading as an honorable contest conducted by rules." It's a case of "may the best contender win." Winning is determined by the individual entrants. In other areas, she has no problem losing, but only occasionally, as she adds, "I wouldn't want to make it a daily habit." She likes winning but always enjoys a race well run.

Mary has learned that she can't do everything. This is a limitation that can be turned into a positive. She knows she has to guard against a stubborn streak that can get her into trouble under certain conditions. She can't do everything at an optimal level even though she'd like to. And although she claims "it's no big deal," doing things well remains a very substantial deal to her. Whatever size the deal is, Mary can handle it. That seems to be what fires her up. Let's not forget that she likes those gauntlets. If outside forces don't produce them, she is capable of supplying her own.

Mary views the market with respect and a certain amount of awe. Its energy and ability to produce a seemingly unending supply of gauntlets cunningly thrown down or subtly left, like quiet clues to be discovered, appeal to her intellectually. She says it's going to go where it wants like a headstrong horse. Her role is to try to anticipate where it's headed and to stay in the saddle. She gets a real charge from making the markets. When she gets there first, it's a definite "kick," to use her word. "It's a great feeling." This confirms her previous observation about the joys of being right. It's being the first one with the answer to a highly complex question. As a challenge, it's like outwitting Jeopardy. It's leading the pack. Mary is definitely not only able to run with the wolves but to lead them. Capably. Skillfully. She develops a good plan that passes all the tests enough of the time and takes her where she wants to go.

———————————————

Mary views the market with respect and a certain amount of awe. Its energy and ability to produce a seemingly unending supply of gauntlets cunningly thrown down or subtly left, like quiet clues to be discovered, appeal to her intellectually.

————————

Mary sees the market and her work as an ever-changing game. Its underlying structure remains basically the same, but the rules and tools are constantly in need of updating as the result of changing market conditions. These changes call for incredible alertness. It's necessary to be ready to change one's plan, no matter how splendid, at the drop of a gauntlet. Then there is perceiving whether it's a real or fake gauntlet!

Mary doubts that she would be able to feel as passionate about another field as she does about this one. "Trading," she says, "satisfies my obsessive/compulsive tendencies and gives me information right away." She is either right or wrong. There is no ambiguity. It is all clear. The other occupation that she could see herself in would be litigation or criminal law. The first fits in well with her verbal dueling skills. The second would use her ability to arrive at the answer, finding clues others missed to solve a complex mystery.

In general, Mary looks for volatility in the market and for underpricing and overpricing. "I try to keep my options open and resist putting on really big positions that are hard to defend or abandon." Any purchase comes with a risk. A good return policy is essential! In some cases, trading is like a military campaign. It is appropriate in this daily struggle to take and hold areas of economic turf, avoiding land mines in the process. Mary plans and executes maneuvers each day. She is a strong advocate of having an opinion on the market but not necessarily "getting stuck on trading with it." An open and clear mind can be alert to changes, positive as well as negative.

In addition, in keeping with her "Scottish economic theory" of buying low and selling high, Mary recommends being "sure that you can do something with what you have." She always tries to use the technical numbers that are there for everyone but that she uses in a different way. This sounds like a recipe for whatever is in the fridge. But it's not!

Physical cues help. Mickey Norton paid attention to what her stomach told her. Mary claims she can smell what "the paper" (the order flow) wants to do. She admonishes traders to keep "poker alert." Eyes and ears open to every subtle twitch so you can learn as much as possible to support your position or take advantage of another option. It's critical to try to "see what other traders are thinking," adding, "Never allow yourself to get shut into a position." Always have a trap door, an emergency escape hatch. Be prepared for worst-case moments and do your best to keep them to a minimum!

Mary's advice to someone thinking about trading as a career choice is to try it out to see if you like it. Theoretically, she believes anyone who wants to do it enough can trade. "You set your own limit and what matters is how much you desire to win." What's really required for the full measure of success is to love it. It's necessary to face and accept those character flaws that are definitely going to appear like a big boil in the middle of the face.

Despite what Mary honestly appraises as a "tough row to hoe," she thoroughly enjoys her work and even goes so far as to admit that "without a doubt" she loves it, especially on good days! There is also no doubt that it's fun, even though it may sound like being boiled in oil to the rest of us. Mary quite literally aches to succeed.

She finds the physical environment, though, leaves much to be desired. It can be pretty nasty, but on the whole it's a fascinating mix of personalities. Mary would recommend it to future daughters or sons only if they "ached" to do it and if they understood what it takes to be successful. "The players are, on the whole, nice and funny." Let's not forget they are all there by choice. Mary's aggressiveness and thirst for competition help her get well positioned at the gate in order to reach the finish line.

Mary is certain that she has learned a great deal from her experiences. She thinks she was very fortunate to be in the right place at the right time. "I think I'm really lucky." She also feels secure with her three pens, always three, in her pocket: two are standard and one is a three-colored musical pen. Why does this suddenly sound like magic? Mary thrives on the routine and believes that arriving equipped for the job with the appropriate mental and physical tools is the ultimate alchemy of trading success.

# CHAPTER 8

# Burning Rubber: The S&P 500

## KATHERINE HARIG

The old expression about staying out of the kitchen if you can't stand the heat certainly applies to the S&P pit, which is where Katherine Harig pits herself on a daily basis at the Chicago Mercantile Exchange (Merc). S&P is short for the Standard and Poor's 500 stock index, which is considered a bellwether for what is happening or is going to happen in the general economy. The stocks in this index are famous for the volatility, unpredictability, and unforgiving speed at which they trade. They draw the cream of the trading talent and only the most skillful make it. Not only has Katherine achieved a place in this financial maelstrom, but she has learned it and worked hard to understand its unruly and constantly changing nature. Trading the S&P has continued to challenge her throughout her 19-year trading career. For all but the past two years, she was at the Chicago office of Goldman Sachs. She started in the S&P pit right out of St. Mary's College where she majored in English and government. After college, Katherine intended to continue on to law school. However, a job as a sales assistant to three institutional salesmen provided her with an entry into the prestigious brokerage firm of Goldman Sachs, one of the giants in the field, which would become her home. Starting from a position as the first phone clerk for Goldman Sach's newly opened commodity floor operation in August 1979. Katherine eventually worked her way up to vice president in charge of the S&P index. She applied for a Merc seat in 1981, started filling orders for the newly trading S&P index the following year, and has never stopped.

Katherine's association with, and attachment to, the S&P goes back to its introduction in 1982 through its infancy and demanding growing years. The S&P is at the tail end of its teenage period and shows no sign of settling down. You can never turn your back on S&P trades. They require total focus and alertness at all times. As Katherine observed, "If you can make it in the S&P, you can make it anywhere!"

Katherine's role in the birth and development of S&P trading has put her in the unique position of understanding the incredible complexity of the index's schizophrenic character. Like the economy itself, the S&P reflects widely diverse market forces that are constantly competing and are subject to multiple volatile influences affecting it in many directions. It is an alive environment characterized by creativity and growth, and fraught with danger and challenge.

———————— ■■■ ————————

Katherine's role in the birth and development of S&P

trading has put her in the unique position of

understanding the incredible complexity of the

index's schizophrenic character.

————

Katherine has never considered another less-taxing trade. She was drawn by the excitement of the S&P floor and likes the feeling of being right at the center of market forces. Information is pouring in, like a waterfall, and you have to sort out the strands that apply and make "money" decisions based on your interpretation of the information. The goal is profit. The information is wasted unless it produces results. It's like connecting a vast tangle of wires that have to be constantly readjusted to achieve and maintain a clear picture that is forever changing focus.

Katherine has been drawn to the S&P with its dense information flow—often fueled by rumor and innuendo. It's a strange amalgam of reality-based intelligence combined with a Shakespearean-like spectacle of human nature in all its varieties. A tall (5 feet 11 inches), slender woman who smiles easily and frequently, Katherine strongly resembles the actress Glenn Close. Although quiet, she assured me her voice carries and she has no trouble making herself heard in the tumultuous market she trades with skillful agility.

A mother of four with children ranging from eight to high school age, Katherine tried staying at home for three years but was pulled back by her professional work. During her years of executing orders for Goldman Sachs, she acquired experience filling both customer orders and the firm's proprietary trading business. This was a valuable learning period when Katherine was given discretion to make trading decisions. "It was a matter of going in and doing it and treating each order as if it were my own money." When Katherine first went into the pit, she felt comfortable with the energy and adrenaline flow of this highly charged market. Katherine does not see the S&P pit as a chaotic situation but focuses on locating and following the beams of information she needs to follow and align herself with. She admits this is easier to do when she is trading and managing money other than her own.

Katherine gives a lot of credit to her boss at Goldman Sachs, John F. Gilmore, who served as her mentor and encouraged her until his retirement, when she made the decision to continue on her own and act as her own mentor. He treated people with dignity and respect and realized that young adults were making large salaries and knew the downfalls that money could bring. He was constantly helping those employees who got caught in the "money trap." She has adopted her former boss's creative outlook on trading and, like him, believes it is more an art than a science. He was someone who understood that mistakes happen because trading is and remains, despite all the technology, a human business. "He expected the best at all times." They enjoyed a mutual respect and, Katherine recalls, her boss was always there to provide backup and support. When Katherine wanted to become the first filling broker in the pit, her boss immediately gave her the go-ahead.

A staggering and constantly shifting array of information that affects the S&P decision-making process is available. The inner circle of this information flow, Katherine informed me, is the men's bathroom which is, of course, off bounds to her. It's not possible for her to be physically privy to the flow of the latest information from the stalls. This humorous but understandable reality is no laughing matter. It definitely affects the evenness of the trading field. Katherine has tried to find a way around this, short of actual invasion. "It pays to have strategically positioned friends in situations like this!"

Katherine's background is solid and quiet. She grew up near Seattle. Her dad was a high school vice principal, as well as a football and track coach, and her mother was and is still a full-time mom. She has seven younger brothers and sisters. Katherine credits her parents with instilling in her a sense of hard work along with high ethical and moral standards. She feels they are the source of her strength. Her previous work experience was limited to J. C. Penney's and a film-processing shop. Katherine was always involved in many school activities, including student government. She enjoys working with people and "getting the job done in the best possible manner."

Katherine recalled the crash of 1987, which, in addition to its broader implications, was an incredible test for the trading industry and its professionals. She remembered the blue-gray atmosphere in the building. It seemed as if there were no lights; they had gone dim. Literally. "The ordeal started on a Friday and didn't seem that bad at first. As the enormity of what was happening became apparent, people either rose to the occasion or, ratlike, abandoned what many perceived as a doomed ship." Katherine remembers canceling a family trip to Hawaii and literally living at her office all weekend. She remembers sleeping (not very much), eating, having her husband bring in fresh clothes, and fearing being pulled out of the pit if her boss found out that she was pregnant (for the third time). "Those who stayed and saw it through demonstrated an extraordinary professionalism and esprit de corps, which showed to the world that even on the darkest day the market would be dealt with in an orderly fashion." The locals stood their ground. A business known for self-interest demonstrated historic cooperation and resilience. Those who were there learned they could count on each other. The experience was incredibly tough, but it strengthened the industry and its players and actually served to promote the business.

When I asked Katherine how she prepares herself for the daily test mentally and physically, she said, "I just get up and go." She has one of many Diet Cokes and takes the train to work from the Chicago suburb where she lives with her family. When Katherine was at Goldman Sachs, she used to read and keep up with all the latest information. Since she has started trading for herself, she relies more on "feel" and intuition from her many years of trading experience. She employs a chartist who provides updates every morning and throughout the day. Talking to other traders and bouncing ideas around also contribute to becoming a better disciplined trader.

Katherine describes herself as quick to react to her rapid-paced work. She also admitted, smiling, "I'm very loud!" She finds her days energizing. If a problem arises, there's no opportunity to brood or delay. "I don't put up with a lot." Whatever comes her way gets cleared up immediately. There's neither time nor energy to waste. Katherine is a Leo who thrives on being in charge and in the middle of the action. "You just have to keep things in perspective, but if something is upsetting it's better to explode and get back to work."

Katherine willingly admits, "I love to win. I hate to lose. I love playing. I love beating the other players just as they enjoy beating me." On a competitive scale, she is a firm ten. Katherine enjoys being part of the extraordinarily talented group of skilled pit traders. She loves to be in control and functions best when "things are organized." Katherine manages to identify and lock on to the information she needs. If the market becomes more chaotic than normal, she steps aside to make rational market decisions. Katherine admits that despite her long trading career for Goldman Sachs, she is just starting out on her own. She is carefully building a solid base and very aware of the danger of ego. The market humbles everyone.

Katherine doesn't have any complicated trading or life rules. Her attitude can best be summed up by saying she has never gone to bed worrying about anything that happened during the trading day, although she has tossed and turned over not following her trading discipline. She has always been ready and able to come back and move on. There have been many best trading moments. In addition to the 1987 crash, the other pivotal event that showed the good character and solid support of so many of her colleagues occurred when one of her children was diagnosed with a life-threatening illness at a young age. She described a moving outpouring of sincere support that included donations of blood, money, and empathy from fellow brokers, locals, and clients.

Bad days on a smaller scale are defused on her train ride home and return to her daily family life and kids' needs. "The market tomorrow is not the market today." Marriage to a "calm and mellow" workaholic husband who is in a different field helps. He keeps their life in balance.

---

Katherine doesn't have any complicated trading or
life rules. Her attitude can best be summed up by
saying she has never gone to bed worrying about
anything that happened during the trading day.

---

Katherine does describe her work as an emotional roller coaster, a virtual bipolar minefield. She admits she is hard on herself and "beats herself up" for not being more aggressive in certain situations. On the other hand, she says, "I don't have to prove anything to anyone." She is there because she thrives on trading's challenges. She took three years off to stay at home with her sick child while he went through chemotherapy but couldn't wait to get back.

She finds family activities help her unwind and maintain her balance: She tries not to miss any of her four children's sports events. She also recharges on family trips to her childhood home on a lake, a virtual "cabin in the woods" with no TV and no radio, where the most important information is what one pine tree is saying to another and the fastest flow is the water in the streams. "You know you can relax when you have to request the business section because it doesn't come with the local paper." Katherine observes that it's easy to get caught up in the "trading culture" and has always preferred to maintain a simple and secure life.

Success is not measured purely in terms of money. A good day is one in which Katherine feels she has gotten "the edge" on the market and participated fully by being in rhythm with the market. The S&P charges to its own complex roar: "You're only as good as your last order filled." And there's the eternal pressing drive forward.

Katherine feels that she gets along well with most of her colleagues in a highly stressful environment. Mutual respect and professional behavior usually gets you through. "I'm always fair." She doesn't believe in backing off. "I'm also very direct. I go to the core." There have been times when she has found herself feeling intimidated by remarks. She recalled one instance when she was pregnant and literally slugged another trader over a rude comment. Both were fined. "It's not very diplomatic to lose your cool." She remembered too the warm baby gifts and congratulations.

Responding to a question about how she sees the market, Katherine observed, "Somebody said it's hell." This seemed an appropriate description of her workplace, which does take a serious toll on the many people who find their weaknesses challenged and unfortunately find themselves engaged in risky behavior or lifestyles. She views trading as a competition requiring everything you've got. Like a field game, there are forces, directions, momentum, and goals to reach. There are winners and losers. There is learning from what happened and using the information in the next trial.

As for the attraction that the market holds, Katherine observed, "It's the flame that all the moths are attracted to." She admitted she doesn't have to work but loves doing it because it puts her in the center of forces that affect and are affected by events around the world. And then there are all those different personalities to deal with!

What helps her find her way is her experience with a market she has been involved with since its inception. Katherine finds she relies a lot on her intuition as well as on her organizational skills. She has the ability to select and "read" order out of the seeming chaos of sound and fury. There is opportunity as well as increased risk in the race-paced S&P. Sometimes the lack of paper causes stalls. Other times, an overabundance results in a dramatic collapse as a "house of cards" loses its delicate balance.

The only other occupation Katherine would find fulfilling and challenging would be coaching girls' basketball or teaching. She enjoys working with people and putting her organizational skills and drive to work to give people opportunities they might not otherwise have. Katherine feels she has been very fortunate in her life and can help others achieve their goals.

When asked if her work is fun, Katherine described it as wonderful fun. "It's the best." She loves it even on the inevitable down days. "I have never not liked it, even on the worst losing day. It is constantly changing. There is always an opportunity to get back on top!" She thrives on the excitement, the amalgam of a vast information network and people coming together with the freedom to achieve something and be their own boss. Last but not least, you don't have to dress up! Katherine's trading career has given her a lot of self-esteem and self-confidence as well as lifelong friendships and connections.

As for recommending the field to someone starting out, Katherine is very positive about the health and growth of the market. She advises, "Respect the people and the market. If you can do that, it's the best. It's not a regular nine-to-five job." Her stamina, height, loud voice, and sense of humor have helped as well. As for future traders among her children, she would have no problem with that if they kept things in perspective. She says her eight-year-old son has the makings of a good trader, and she is quite certain he will become one. He is very good at math, is interested in what she does, and gives her suggestions that he expects her to follow to make a profit! He's usually right.

Katherine is not superstitious but doesn't believe in tempting fate. "I always take the same seat on the train, enter through the same turnstile, and walk on to the floor the same way!" As for doing it all over again: "Definitely."

# CHAPTER 9

# The Matchmaker from Minsk

JENNIFER STRAUSBERG

Jennifer Strausberg is an Energizer bunny. She doesn't take "no" as an answer, and she never stops until she gets what she wants. She is indefatigable, creative, funny, and extremely good at what she does, and she thoroughly enjoys her work. A former trader who has gone beyond trading, she has turned networking into an art form that is her modus operandi.

Her path has been about as linear as architect Frank Gehry's designs. She grew up in a small town in woodsy upstate New York, an area she humorously compares to the movie *Deliverance*. Her father is a federal mediator and her mother an interior designer. Interestingly, her parents remember Jennifer successfully mediating the inevitable disputes that make up so much of the social fabric of childhood. This early training in dealing with different personalities and working toward a mutually acceptable conclusion has contributed substantially to her present career.

She was selected by the Rotary Exchange Program to spend her senior year of high school in Japan. This experience was an eye-opening one that left an enduring mark on her. It gave her a global perspective and an adaptability to, and skill at accepting, other viewpoints. When she came home, she took a year off to find a direction. After working at a Japanese-owned steel minimill in New York State, Jennifer entered Parsons School of Design to work toward a degree in package design. This effort came to an abrupt end when she searched her soul in her junior year and concluded that she was making a poor "life investment" whose return would take years to realize. "I was wasting my time." She was utterly convinced that she had other worlds, besides packaging, to conquer. Despite the concern of her parents, this decision turned out to be very productive. Package design's loss was the business world's gain.

Jennifer's talent for networking began to surface when she used her experience at the minimill as well as her year in Japan to see a business connection between a Japanese steel producer and a Korean seaweed plant. Not obvious but it worked and encouraged her to continue.

Some pursue their dreams on Broadway, but Jennifer headed to Wall Street where she secured an entry-level job as a runner in the gold market. "I hated it." Interestingly enough, she not only works on Wall Street now but lives in the area as well. Her next position was as an interbank broker, arranging financial transactions between major banks. "I am not one to let grass grow under my feet." After that, she traded "repos," the acronym for repurchase (mortgage) agreements, for Prudential Bache. Always ready to handle more than one task at a time, Jennifer met her husband, a commodities trading adviser, while on an interview at Nikko Securities. "He decided I would make a better wife than his trading assistant."

Next, she was moved into raising and managing money. This period of "meeting and greeting" helped her widen her net and hone her skill of creating and promoting goodwill between parties. She is a people person who derives tremendous satisfaction from bringing people together in the business environment. Hence her nickname for herself, "the matchmaker from Minsk." "I have a great time (doing my work), meeting so many interesting people, and getting all kinds of information." Her job is to figure out ways of bringing different information together in a synergistic relationship.

Jennifer's ability to focus and act swiftly was fostered by her trading experience. Although the possibility that she is "going to step on a rake" is always present, she is confident of her abilities. "I have never told myself that I can't do something. I've always been a go-getter." She is overflowing with energy and is "very persistent," actually "stubborn" in her pursuit of her goals. She is off the competitive scale, ten or beyond. "My work has taught me that I can do it. I can pretty much do anything I want."

---

"I have never told myself that I can't do something.

I've always been a go-getter."

---

Jennifer has a phone virtually growing as an extension to her ear. She keeps in contact with her network via phone and e-mail. This self-described "neurotic list maker" and heavy Post-it note user has a very inclusive style and expansive outlook. Jennifer also believes in a light touch along with the ability to laugh at herself. We exchanged some humor by e-mail that was going to be passed on to a Swiss business connection. Her design background helps her find creative solutions to "business deal design" and "packaging." Much of her business is sealed with her word and a handshake. And, according to her, "I do not gossip."

She has a reputation for following through, dealing fairly, and avoiding the draining tendency to get bogged down in time-consuming and unproductive, unimportant minutiae.

Jennifer's basic rule for life, as well as for work, is, in her words, "Constantly try to network." She remembers her mother's advice that you catch more flies with honey than with vinegar.

When Jennifer feels the need to take a break from her pressure-driven career, "I go off to Israel where I can be a vegetable on a beach." She has also participated in archeological digs on biblical sites, an activity that she finds puts everything in perspective and connects her to ancient times and ideas. She converted to Judaism when she married her husband and has a very strong attachment to it, peppering her conversation with Yiddish phrases and giving generously to Jewish charities and Hebrew University.

A daily means of relaxing is doing "home stuff" with her young daughter and husband who is a fixed-income bond trader, not exactly a low-key occupation. As we were talking, she was making dinner. In fact, a major interest of hers is cooking, a skill that is transferred to the innovative ways Jennifer "mixes" and combines people and their business ideas. She feels it's critical to vent and get it all out by doing something positive. She also finds aerobics and weight training help her maintain her high-energy level. In addition, she enjoys flower arranging, listening to jazz, and reading.

Jennifer is extremely positive. "There has been a lot of good stuff." More than once she quoted Hamlet's advice to Horatio, "There is more under heaven and earth than thy philosophy ever dreamt of," to illustrate the unexpected turns life takes. One such personal event was learning she had cervical cancer two months before her marriage and that she could never have children. She did get married, did have a child, and is enjoying great health. One reason for her tremendous productivity and energy is the awareness that you never know when a brick will fall on your head.

Jennifer believes in doing everything possible to turn a negative into a positive. She doesn't find it productive to dwell on a negative but prefers to view any negative as a challenge. There is always someone or something ready to divert one from the goal. Her response to a loss is to try to pull back and reassess the situation and attack the problem from another angle. "There are always difficulties. I prioritize. I stay focused. I just do it." She admits she is a classic driven type A personality.

A successful day for Jennifer is a really busy one when the phones are ringing and the faxes are streaming in from all over. The switchboard is lit up. The voice mail and call waiting are packed. "I'm running!" She's going down her lists, making strategic moves and decisions that activate her worldwide network of contacts.

Jennifer is accustomed to dealing on a high professional level with major business forces and major CEOs. She finds she gets along very well with men but feels she can be viewed as a threat by women who feel intimidated or insecure. This is someone who combines gray flannel with lace and likes a good cigar. She does admit to feelings of intimidation on occasion. Jennifer recalled carrying an Exacto blade when she was a subway-riding art student but, she says, "I never had to use it."

If you are getting an impression of someone who likes to be in control, you are absolutely correct. "I always have to drive. . . . I know how to get there." She admits that "we have had our moments" in 12 years of marriage.

Jennifer's other relationship has been her work, which she describes as "having fun." She sees her role as the matchmaker who brings the couple together and helps create a successful bond.

"Totally nuts" is how Jennifer characterizes herself. Also adaptable and never still. She approaches any business situation well prepared and confident. "I arm myself with as much information as possible." She is highly skilled at unorthodox "thinking on my feet."

---

"I arm myself with as much information as possible."

---

Jennifer's strength comes from her total engagement with whatever she is doing. "From a young age I always believed I was destined for bigger and better things. I've never settled for less." She has high standards that she is constantly meeting and exceeding. When she didn't like the way her life was going, she always realized it was up to her to make a change.

She has no second career choice or interest. "I'm having way too much fun." Jennifer derives tremendous satisfaction from seeing her carefully designed plans, incorporating diverse elements, dovetail and coalesce. "I can't imagine doing anything else!" A successful business venture resembles the final scene in a Shakespearean comedy where everyone is finally matched up, everyone has a role that suits him or her, and life goes on to the next scene.

---

Jennifer's advice to anyone contemplating following her: "Expect to work very hard; you have to like it or you won't be able to work hard enough."

---

The personal quality that she finds helps her best is a dauntless spirit of adventure and goal-orientedness. If one way doesn't work, she is the one to figure out another way. The whole deal can usually be diagrammed by her "feir kashes" or four questions:

1. What's in it for me?
2. What's in it for you?

3.  Why do you need me?
4.  Why do I need you?

Jennifer's advice to anyone contemplating following her: "Expect to work very hard; you have to like it or you won't be able to work hard enough." She wants her daughter to do whatever makes her happy: Broadway, Wall Street, or some other path.

What she really loves about her work is not primarily the money, although that *is* the means of keeping score. Jennifer is drawn by the traveling and meeting an incredibly diverse array of people. She finds her work exciting and interesting and is always extending its reach. Her business questions focus on what makes others tick, what makes them happy. It's the basic material of human nature. Whatever she does, she is never too busy to send a personal note to follow up a business meeting or conversation. Jennifer is always willing to go the extra distance to get it right. Her philosophy can be summed up thus: "Some days you're the windshield; some days you're the bug." There are not many bug days for her.

---

Her philosophy can be summed up thus: "Some days
you're the windshield; some days you're the bug."
There are not many bug days for her.

---

It has taken her some time to figure out what she's doing and she feels she's just hitting her stride. She doesn't try to pretend to know everything but is always willing to learn and be flexible. "I love to cut to the chase." The day after we spoke she was on her way to Italy to look at a handful of emeralds to see if she wanted to locate a buyer within her network.

# CHAPTER 10

# The Art of a Trader

## ANN BERG

My first impression of Ann Berg was through her quiet English-accented voice, which she comes by naturally from her mother. She sounded, in a word, competent. She had just returned from a trip to Turkey on behalf of the United Nations where she was an adviser on the establishment of a modern grain exchange that would be able to compete on a global level. She faxed me her impressive résumé, which was dense with evidence of her thorough knowledge of, and performance in, the futures industry, where she has specialized in grains. It took several readings just to absorb its depth and breadth. Her grain of choice is corn. She knows everything about it and has first-hand experience in storing and shipping to hedging, arbitraging, and conducting cost and risk analyses. Ann has a place in the trading annals as the first female grain exporter in the world. "I have done everything associated with corn, including personally planting and harvesting it."

We met at the Chicago Board of Trade (CBOT) where she has served two terms as a director. She is one of two women in the history of the CBOT to hold this position with its considerable responsibilities and prestige. I made my way to the gleaming glass floor-to-ceiling annex, which resembles a sculpture more than an office space. My impression was of a glass silo, a storage facility for speculative capital collecting here with museum orderliness from financial centers around the globe.

---

Ann has a place in the trading annals as the first female grain exporter in the world. "I have done everything associated with corn, including personally planting and harvesting it."

---

Ann Berg is a small, lively woman with delicate but strong features and whose crisp, articulate speech suggests her mother's England more than her father's Minnesota. She apologized for keeping me waiting even though it was for a very short time. We found an empty room and began the interview.

I had an impression of someone who studies something in depth until she understands it completely. Her blue eyes are direct and appeared to be gathering information as we spoke. She was accustomed, I kept thinking, to observing all manner of individual grains and calculating how they fit together.

Ann's early interest in grain grew out of her lawyer-father's involvement in a lawsuit brought by a grain exchange. After graduating from Carlton College with a sociology-anthropology major, her knowledge of grain led to a job with the international firm Louis-Dreyfus where she worked with a London-educated Jamaican and learned as much as she could about the business.

She went on to Philipp Brothers, another global firm, where she helped design and establish its grain division. She finally arrived at the Chicago Board of Trade, where she was backed by a young speculator.

Recently, Ann has expanded her vistas by consulting at the invitation of the United Nations as part of its effort to promote risk management solutions in developing nations. Ann has found it tremendously gratifying to put her store of knowledge to work in such a critical area. She is very interested in maximizing resources in order to help achieve global food security.

It is impossible to overestimate the importance of grain in the world. It might put things in perspective if we remember that just about all of the world's people consume some form of grain daily. Ann sees her emerging consultant's role as instrumental in the creation of a sound market policy for global food security. It has led to her speaking at international conferences in Rome, Brussels, Washington, D.C., and at the United Nations in New York as well as serving on economic missions to Turkey.

Ann learned to trade as she learned everything else in life. "I always did my homework and made sure I was well prepared." She studied the fundamentals and made disciplined information-based decisions designed to uncover or take advantage of an opportunity.

The quality that she has really been able to rely on has been her uncompromising tenacity. There is no point in leaving a muskrat half-skinned (more about that later)! Ann believes the capacity to reevaluate a situation on the basis of changing information is crucial. There is always something new coming in that changes the basic dynamic.

Her involvement with the United Nations and global economics is firmly grafted onto her reappraisal of trading's role in her life. Ann has an ironic view. Both her trading and her serving on the CBOT's board of directors spawned her unforgettable observation on the potential and periodically considered merger of the Board of Trade and the Chicago Mercantile Exchange as "square dancing with her cross-eyed cousins." This humorous phrase describes the prospective reality of working with people who see things differently, perhaps less globally. She is interested in solving a problem and will enter a maelstrom if she has to whether it's trading corn or working with a United Nations mission in a critical area.

---

Both her trading and her serving on the CBOT's board of directors spawned her unforgettable observation on the potential and periodically considered merger of the Board of Trade and the Chicago Mercantile Exchange as "square dancing with her cross-eyed cousins."

---

Ann believes her problem-solving skills were enhanced by having a mother who was drafted into the British army during World War II. Her mother served as a cryptographer, working 16-hour shifts in Churchill's famous underground war room. She came to Minnesota as a GI bride and settled down to her new life as a lawyer's wife.

Ann's early work experience is as unique as her subsequent career and certainly indicated an interest and ability to get beneath the surface. At the ages of eight, nine, and ten she was doing a lot more than reading adventure stories or arranging doll houses. Ann was out trapping and skinning muskrats and other small game. She described the technique: Cut a circle and then peel the skin like a grape. She was paid a dollar for each pelt. She also harvested wild rice, shingled and tar-papered roofs, designed and built furniture, and laid concrete! She is certainly well rounded and has a hauntingly superb curriculum vitae. "I get my self-reliance from my father. He believed in using both hands. In doing a 'full job.'"

Ann's guiding advice to anyone contemplating trading as a career is "to thine own self be true," stay healthy, and get enough sleep. Trading is extremely draining work.

Ann observed that "there are no guarantees in life." She describes herself as a cynic and, at the same time, an optimist, an interesting mix. She has chosen a path that has taken her to the top of her chosen field. She is fervently independent and has never married. Perhaps she is unwilling to compromise her professional life for domestic concerns in somebody else's version of Minnesota. She has, in a way, also devoted her professional life to decoding problems, to seeing complex data clearly.

There have been times, of course, when she hasn't seen things clearly and the day doesn't go as planned. Ann's response to loss is to not keep going and hope the loss will iron itself out. "In certain circumstances all you can do is shut down." When she has lost "enough money," it's time to exit. She stops trading to give herself a chance to review the situation and see if she is making a strategic error. Sometimes it's not so much a misjudgment in trading style as it is a matter of being out of step. Perhaps there's been a change in market rhythm or timing.

Success to Ann is not measured by the number of times the cash register jingles. "The respect of my peers is very important." She has certainly accumulated evidence of respect, having been elected to the CBOT board and chosen to represent the CBOT on various committees and international missions. She does admit that success in trading has made it possible for her to do a little shopping or, better yet, spend time in her favorite stress-reducing location, Rome.

Ann has gotten along with her colleagues just fine. As long as all are doing their job and fulfilling their professional role, things tend to go smoothly. Sometimes, though, "behavior can become rather primitive." She did recall one occasion when two traders "got into it" and actually drew blood. In fact, one bit off a piece of the other's ear! The following day they were back, one with a bandage covering

27 stitches, working right alongside each other. "The previous day was gone. It was a new day presenting opportunities that couldn't be missed, ear or no ear!"

There have been occasions when Ann has felt intimidated by large groups of male traders when she is the sole woman. With repeated practice and experience speaking before large groups on behalf of the futures industry, Ann believes feeling intimidated has become less of a problem.

She is fond of being in control of knowledge. She feels things go better when she is functioning in a decision-making capacity. She is careful to explain that what she is referring to is not the crazed megalomaniacal form of control but the reasoned, information-based, and experience-supported variety that leads to productive decisions and successful outcomes.

As for being competitive, Ann sees herself scoring high, a 10 on a scale of 1 to 10. She is especially good at anything involving the pursuit of knowledge or words. She plays no sports but does ride a stationary bicycle in front of the TV.

She describes her relationship to the market as that of a student. There is always more knowledge to gain. The market is always teaching. As in life, you have to be willing and available to learn and then be prepared to apply your knowledge.

---

What Ann looks for in a market is intimately connected with her method of problem solving. This unique journey to a solution—her particular truth— can be best understood through her art. Ann is an extremely accomplished artist.

What Ann looks for in a market is intimately connected with her method of problem solving. This unique journey to a solution—her particular truth—can be best understood through her art. Ann is an extremely accomplished artist.

Her art, however, is not easy to categorize in the usual way. When I finally saw her work, I was deeply moved, even astonished. As a professional artist, I would like to say with humility I feel qualified to describe these extraordinary works. To my way of thinking, they are journeys from dark to light. Ann builds them slowly and carefully on paper, using printmaking techniques in conjunction with pastels, words, even pieces of found paper, such as corners torn from old street posters. The series I saw was based on Dante's *Inferno*. Each picture was like an illustration from the pages of one of the world's great works of literature. There was so much to see. There were layerings of color, of changing values of light and dark. The abstract was combined with the representational. The pictures were full of passion and absolute dedication to the struggle to pass through the dark and reach the light. Ann has been exhibited and it was clear to me that she could be a successful, recognized artist if she so chose.

The movement from dark to light that appears in her art is also revealed in her work method, which can best be described as the deciphering of a dark problem, bringing the light of knowledge and experience to its ultimate resolution.

Her reputation as a problem solver with a clear gaze has brought her to the attention of a group of grain producers in Canada who need help with a complex matter involving their industry. She has been called in as a sort of Sherlock Holmes, an expert witness, the best they could think of.

What Ann brings to a problem is an ability to work until she clearly understands the underlying structural framework. This is evident in examples of her artistic expression as well as in her professional history as a trader. She sifts through all the layers to the final essence that brings understanding. It is like a dance of art and mathematics. This may seem paradoxical until we remember that Picasso and other great artists saw both the figurative, abstract, and practical possibilities inherent in numbers.

Ann describes herself as tenacious. This doggedness doesn't allow her to give up until she has reached her objective. It has helped her in skinning muskrats, in creating her works of art, and in her problem-solving style of trading.

Qualities that Ann feels are inhibiting are her feelings of failure as well as her fear of failure. These feelings are hardly surprising in someone who sets extremely high standards for herself. It takes a lot to measure up to them. Ann sees herself as bold and direct in trading as well as in life. "I demand a lot from myself and get it." Ann has "being independent" down, or rather "up," to a high art. "The downside is that I spend a great deal of time alone." Work can be very draining and often, after a long day, there is only enough energy remaining to leaf through magazines.

If Ann chose another career, it would be art. She also enjoys serving as an expert financial consultant, which requires another kind of creativity. Ann sees the world's markets as driven by fear and greed and sees her role as more of an integrative one in which she tries to do some good on a national or global level, such as the mission to Turkey and her work in Canada. Ann believes it's important that whatever you do satisfies your soul.

Walking, recreation, exercise, and conversation with great friends help her unwind and restore herself. She also designs and sews exquisite clothes. The day we met she was wearing a blue coat she had made for herself from Italian cashmere. The inside was beautifully finished, like a fine couture garment. Ann told me some of her design ideas are based on her printmaking and her love of color. She looks forward to traveling, especially to spending extended periods of time in Rome. Ann often feels that her life needs "more Rome and less Chicago."

When asked what she thought of the prevalent comparison males make between trading and sex or war, she said she could see why they would see it in those ways. She thought it was definitely more than "just getting lucky on a date"! She views it more like a giant complex canvas on which often conflicting ideas are played out. She feels trading has a very real physical nature as well. "It can be thrilling but also enraging and frightening." This is an observation from someone who doesn't especially like crowds to begin with!

Trading has provided Ann with a great living and financial independence. Although she lives quietly, preferring to sew or paint, many choices are available to her that make trading worthwhile and rewarding.

Trading has kept her life simpler as she oscillates between buying and selling decisions. As a position trader, Ann takes her work home and admitted she would feel naked if she didn't have a position to think about. She is also concerned about whether "her life is living her."

Asked which of her personal qualities served her best, she felt she relied most on her intelligence and instinct. Those muskrat-skinning days provided valuable training. "You never want to put yourself, or have circumstances place you, in the muskrat's position." If the trade doesn't smell right, there is probably a good reason why you shouldn't do it. "I have seen too many people go for broke and get there," Ann observed. "You always want to move out of the dark, the area of insufficient knowledge, and into the light, the place of knowledge and reason."

Ann's advice to anyone considering trading would be to get training and experience from inside a company or a large corporation. She recommends a mentor who is a good personal match. It should be an individual who can serve as a guide for teaching you the trails and ways of the financial terrain you are entering as well as someone with whom you feel a connection.

She has found her trading career fun and has enjoyed her work despite occasional periodic frustrations. And she admits "trading used to be more gratifying before the markets changed." Undercapitalized individuals are no match against deep-pocketed institutional traders.

Ann has spent 25 years in the industry and her intelligence, experience, and knowledge of all aspects of her field are welcomed in the international consulting markets.

Nothing has been wasted in her life. Every bit of knowledge, paint, paper, or cloth has been applied with precision and imagination. If you plan carefully and know what you're doing, always thinking as you go along, there shouldn't be any large leftover heaps of scraps and unusable material. Ann has achieved an underlying framework in her life that reflects her ceaseless search through darkness or ignorance for the light of knowledge. Her goal in her business career, as in her art and life, has been to achieve a transparency, where it is possible to understand how all the different elements form an integrated whole.

Despite the changes she has seen in the markets and her own internal compass shifts, she would do it all over again but would compress the 20 years into a compact 10. During the course of our interview, Ann revealed that the animal she could most identify with was the cheetah. Just as a cheetah covers the ground in an economy of concentrated bright energy, I can see her performing a similar leap in the financial markets and in her future challenges.

# CHAPTER 11

# Lion Trader

**SHARON KING**

The day I called Sharon King to arrange for an interview she told me the following day wasn't going to work out because she was taking her grandmother to get a new pair of eyeglasses. I immediately had a favorable impression of a woman who had her priorities centered around people she cared about. This was born out by her story, which I heard the following day.

Sharon ambled into the art gallery I run at the conclusion of her trading day at the Chicago Board Options Exchange (CBOE), where she has spent nine years. She is currently trading options and stocks of such companies as Amoco, Corning Glass, Avon, Bristol Meyers, and Champion. She looked like someone just getting off the graveyard shift of an air traffic control tower, an ER, or a cab route. There was a comfortable nonchalance about her manner that said she had just completed a well-done job and was ready to take on the next assignment. She beamed a big smile and greeted me warmly. Her trading jacket was slung over her arm like the warm-up jacket of a national champion.

Sharon probably has as many unique qualities as she has lucky pins on her trading jacket. She is African American for one, the only black trader at her level at the CBOE. When I asked about other African-American women in the industry, she said there were some working as brokers and clerks but as far as she knew she was the only one in Chicago who was an independent trader. She also had no knowledge of African-American women at other exchanges. Sharon is very much a "no big deal" kind of person and does not need identification beyond herself.

---

Sharon probably has as many unique qualities as she has lucky pins on her trading jacket.

---

Sharon was not dealt a good hand when she started life. In fact, you could say her cards were cruelly taken away from her when her young mother was murdered. Her mother had tried to break up a bad romantic relationship, but things got out of control. Her boyfriend shot her and, afraid no one would believe his claim that it was an accident, turned the gun on himself, with fatal consequences. Sharon was six and went to live with her maternal grandmother, the one who later got the glasses. To put it mildly, it was not easy! Sharon also had a sister who had juvenile diabetes and needed constant care. Her sister is waiting for a lifesaving kidney replacement and remains one of Sharon's symbols of courage.

Sharon has very fond memories of her time with her grandmother; they have always been emotionally close. Sharon remembers with affection her grandmother's stories and her habits, such as warming her hands by holding boiled eggs. Sharon is convinced that she got her strong personality from her grandmother, who also let Sharon know that she believed in her. She conveyed to her granddaughter that she needed to accept help when it was offered and to take that help and go somewhere with it so those who extended it would be proud of her. She also got across the message that sooner or later you have to help yourself. Sharon's most memorable regret about growing bigger was that she couldn't sit on her grandmother's lap anymore!

Sharon remembers that she was always using her mind. She didn't have much materially, but she did have her mind, and it has always gotten a good workout. Her grandmother was unable to afford the telescope she wanted for Christmas but managed to give her a microscope instead. Sharon wasn't disappointed. Instead of looking out, she began looking in. Her grandmother also got her a set of encyclopedias. To this day she enjoys just opening up a volume and reading. She has a very open mind that is always ready to learn and willing to expand. "Learning makes you richer."

Sharon was not much of a doll player. "I preferred to play with the little green soldiers, like the ones in the movie *Toy Story*." She spent a lot of time reading and was particularly drawn to history. She remembers reading *The Autobiography of Malcolm X* when she was still in grammar school. Sharon prefers facts. Fiction really has to grab her, though she did manage to get through *The Color Purple*.

Her life changed abruptly once more during her youth and again she had to adapt to a major alteration in her fortunes. When her resources and responsibilities were stretched to the breaking point, her grandmother had to make the hard choice to place Sharon in an orphanage until circumstances improved. Many of Sharon's friends had turned to drugs when they were teenagers and her grandmother wanted Sharon in a safer place. In retrospect, Sharon thought it was a good move "away from the negative energy of the streets."

Sharon found herself in a facility named Angel Guardian, a place whose inhabitants she has interestingly come to consider as her second family. She has never borne any resentment against her grandmother for giving her up as many others might easily have done. Although she does describe Angel Guardian as a "nice place," she also admits that some kids there had "adult problems." Sharon was determined to make the most of this experience "as my grandmother had taught me." What could easily have been another devastating event in her life was turned into a positive opportunity for making something of herself and getting on with her life in a world that seemed to deliver her one crummy blow after another.

At Angel Guardian Sharon was taken under the wing of a kindly priest who served as the male role model she was lacking. Father Daniel McCarthy was her coach on the basketball court and on the playing field of life. This sounds like pure Hollywood and reminds me of Bing Crosby's role in the film classic *Boys Town*. As Sharon says, "I always worked hard and always listened. I remember his love of free throws and free thinking, despite his rigorous religion."

While at Angel Guardian Sharon was cocaptain of the girls' softball team, which won the Chicago city championship. For a long time, she held the record for the highest batting average in the city. Winning left a great taste in Sharon's mouth. She had played a major role in the victory and felt poised for new challenges.

She remembers that when Father McCarthy talked about the religious troubles in Ireland, she told him that she had never before heard of white people fighting each other. Angel Guardian's population was diverse and included whites, blacks, and Hispanics. Sharon said it reminded her of the old Pat Boone movie *The Cross and the Switch Blade*. She remembers dressing in a white shirt and neat skirt for mass, going home for Thanksgiving and Christmas, and her grandmother's monthly visits.

Change was a constant in Sharon's young life. The diocese closed Angel Guardian, and she was moved to a group home staffed by women who she recalls lacked "high school degrees." There she remembers ordering pizzas and beer. At one point she was actually threatened with prison "on charges that I didn't clean up my room and was acting obnoxious." In other words, Sharon was behaving like a normal teenager. She saved herself with the help of a science teacher, Mary Carey, who became her foster mother. "Besides being white, she was very kind and understanding and treated me like a daughter." Unlike others Sharon knew, she never ran away. "Remember," Sharon told me, "after what happened to my mother, I never knew if it was the last time I was going to see someone that I cared for."

Mary Carey was someone Sharon felt she could always talk to. At this time of her life, Sharon wanted to be an astronaut. The mere lack of a telescope was not enough to make her change her sights! In high school she made the honor roll. After graduating, Sharon attended Loyola for a year on a government scholarship. She recalls that all the guys lived on campus, but the girls had to walk four or five blocks to their dorms! She took a year off from her studies to work and never returned to school. She landed a job that probably taught her a great deal more than the business courses Loyola offered.

The father of one of her teachers at Angel Guardian was the vice chairman at the Chicago Board Options Exchange and helped her get a job as a price reporter. She worked her way up the personnel ladder, always thinking to herself that she wanted to do what the traders were doing, which seemed to resemble playing sports while earning a rich living.

There was no question in her mind that in trading or sports, "If guys could do it, so could I." But how? Sharon remembers softball games the girls played against the boys at Angel Guardian that sometimes lasted 12 innings. A game, no matter how long, was just another opportunity for victory!

The trading floor was but one more new situation to adapt to if Sharon was going to survive. She credits the orphanage and group home along with her foster home experience with giving her the ability to develop her organizational skills as well as teaching her how to get along with a diverse group of personalities, working together as a unit. "Trading," Sharon observed, "was certainly easier than scrubbing floors at the group home." The CBOE was an environment she instantly recognized: diverse and challenging. Instead of unruly kids, she was faced with traders. Instead of starting over, Sharon viewed trading as just another move, an opportunity to do something "I was preparing to do all my life."

———————■———————

The trading floor was but one more new situation to

adapt to if Sharon was going to survive. She credits

the orphanage and group home along with her

foster home experience with giving her the ability to

develop her organizational skills as well as teaching

her how to get along with a diverse group

of personalities.

————

Sharon learned by talking to people, studying tapes, and taking seminars that the exchange offered to its employees. She was confident and committed to learning how to play this new game. "I never stopped asking questions." Sharon is a fervent learner and believes there are no stupid questions. She credits another woman on the floor, Sarah Harmon Phillips, for encouraging her and never tiring of providing answers. "If you want to survive and prevail, you can never stop learning. Who would want to!"

She also credits Tom Haugh with providing her with her first real break on the floor. He was her coach on a softball team of CBOE women and she ended up on his "trading" team a few years later, progressing from clerk to floor manager to trader.

Sharon practices an active kind of listening. She says basic listening is not enough, especially in complex situations such as the trading environment. Normal listening is just the beginning. She stresses the critical importance and value of active hearing, which makes sense of what is being communicated and helps promote understanding of the "disorganized confusion." Let's face it, without knowledge and understanding, life itself appears to be "disorganized confusion."

Sharon's persistent questions sought to figure out what was going on. What she first considered disorganized confusion Sharon gradually began to see as increasingly less confused and more highly organized procedures. Although she does admit there are days when disorganized confusion is an accurate description for what's going on!

Another experience that helped Sharon was a summer job as a camp counselor where she was entrusted with 40 boys, aged 7 to 12, from nine to four every day. The parallels to traders and the exchange environment widened her ever-present smile.

Sharon recalls her first day trading. She lost $250 at the opening. "It was gone in a minute." She was feeling as down as her pocketbook until she said to herself the day had just begun and she had six hours to make it back. "I'm not the sort of person to let money disappear. I've worked too hard. I also knew that just because you foul at the beginning of a game doesn't prevent you from making a basket later on."

That day she made back the money and then some! Sharon is someone who sees the glass as half full and doesn't see any point in letting any water go to waste! She is dedicated to filling that glass up to the top. "It can even go over!"

Plainly speaking, Sharon has an incredibly positive outlook. Experiences that might have been viewed as permanent life disablers Sharon got through with a strong will and inner confidence that has always served her well in all situations. Her time at Angel

Guardian was a defining time in her life that helped build her strong character and fostered a personal discipline and dedication to survive on her terms.

Sharon describes herself as a "people person" who is interested in, and able to form relationships with, whomever she finds herself with. She believes that success is all about "getting exposure." "You can't hide from life. It's going to find you, so you might as well do a good job." Sharon adds, "Learning as much as you can keeps everything oiled and a full tank of gas helps!"

For Sharon, the unexpected and tragic loss of her mother fostered an appreciation of her fellow human beings. Rather then being embittered, she has an almost Falstaffian generosity of spirit and soul that is apparent to anyone who spends time with her. She is extremely good company. She is articulate, smart, funny, and has a wicked sense of humor. Although we were meeting for the first time, the interview time flew by like a conversation with an old friend.

———————————————

For Sharon, the unexpected and tragic loss of her mother fostered an appreciation of her fellow human beings. Rather then being embittered, she has an almost Falstaffian generosity of spirit and soul that is apparent to anyone who spends time with her.

————————

Sharon prepares herself for trading's daily demands by "being my own positive self and remembering that the glasses are half full and in need of topping off." Life is too short for anything else and she makes a conscious effort to remove herself from situations or people charged with "negative energy." Saying "can" will get you to go that extra inch when sometimes it's the only difference between success and failure. If Sharon loses a little money, she views it as spilling a little water that she knows she'll have the opportunity to get back the next day.

It is extremely inspirational to listen to her speak with utter sincerity and from her life's experiences. She is charismatic. Given different circumstances, I can see her having a following. What she says clearly makes sense and she is living proof of its value.

Sharon says she basically does what she wants to do. Her positive outlook doesn't have room for wringing her hands or wallowing in self-pity. Sharon confided with a chuckle that she and her grandmother aren't prejudiced, "we hate everybody equally!" Yes, they're kidding. She doesn't believe in wasting energy on hate when she can increase it by doing something positive.

At five o'clock Sharon called the exchange for her technical numbers, monitoring the market activity that would affect her game plan for the following day. She resumed our talk with the smile. Her positions were all working out.

Sharon claims her "street smarts" help her trade. She's got "eyes in the back of my head and instinct tells me to avoid alleys and dead ends, real and financial." You have to be smart but a Ph.D. isn't a passport to success. No matter what kind of a day it is, she firmly believes there's always hope. But hope needs help, which translates as developing a trading plan and following it. Sharon believes in luck as making the most of a well-planned situation but doesn't believe in waiting to win the lottery. She has a great phrase that expresses this philosophy: "I'd rather be a player than a prayer!"

When faced with some form of "disorganized confusion" on the floor or in life, she has always been one to take a deep breath and examine what's going on around her. She does not fall prey to the stampede mentality. Sharon has learned it's better to find out if there actually is a fire before getting stuck in the exit with everyone else trying to get out. In trading, as in sports and life, "It's better to figure out plays and be prepared so you're not caught with your pants off or your trading jacket on inside out."

Trading has confirmed what Sharon's life experiences had already taught her. She knew she could do it. Once she had that badge on, there was no stopping her.

She is not an extravagant woman and says she has "everything a poor man wants"! She has put her money into a house, where she enjoys puttering around. "If a man can do it, I can do it!" Sharon claims she has a "brown thumb" and plants should keep their distance if they want to go on living. She admits she has a weakness for electronic gadgets. A big-screen TV was waiting for her handy uncle to help her install. She drives an inexpensive car and has been known to take the train to work.

She is a private person who is quietly generous with her family and friends. As she says, she is the one who picks up the check. She has no plans to marry because it is hard to find a good human being, but that hasn't stopped her from being involved. She has helped three nieces and one nephew get summer jobs at the exchange and is very pleased that two of them are considering it as a career option. She remains very close to her family.

Her trading rules are like her life rules. You never know what tomorrow or the next hour or even minute will bring. Take everything a day, an hour, or a minute at a time. She chided herself for starting to get upset about something until she heeded her own advice. Sharon believes in practicing diplomacy and avoids the male ego-driven "cock wars" that trading pits are famous for.

As far as moments that stand out, she quoted the well-known phrase, "Everything's funny when you're making money." Her worst moment is the flip side, any time she's losing money. She does whatever it takes to "end the pain" of losing. Sharon always tries to turn a loser into a winner, a negative into a positive. She has no interest in being "a prayer" and will go all out to remain "a player."

Sharon says trading is her job. Pressure is what you put on yourself. As she observed, driving a CTA bus can be stressful. She is a "back spreader," which in her case means she can be up or down big. It goes with the territory. She doesn't like to be short "premium."

Sharon handles loss by having a "guardian angel" on her shoulder. This reminder of her past is a small gold pin attached to the lapel of her trading jacket that leads a column of pewter pins, each of which has special meaning for her. There is Marvin the Martian, chosen because he was the only black cartoon character she could find. She relaxes by watching cartoons and enjoys the character of Marvin because he is convinced he is going to rule the world despite the fact that he is "always getting his ass kicked." A little lesson in life to help her through the day.

Next on her lapel is a National Rifle Association pin, a gift from a friend. It also signifies that "good people should be able to protect themselves." A bear reaching into a honey pot suggests her view of trading and life. "Life should be sweet. It's not easy to get that honey and avoid being stung." The latest one is a little elephant, Ganesha, an Indian deity who is the remover of obstacles and the patron god of prosperity and creativity. Sharon believes "you make your luck but when fortune smiles on you, it can't hurt to smile back." A good day is today. If it's not, do something immediately to limit that pain. When she loses money, she's just down and it's not the end of the world. "It's not cancer." For Sharon, every day is a good day. She tries to make every day well lived and well worked.

Success is being comfortable with what you've chosen to do with your life. She tries to keep things in perspective. Keeping positive does not mean going out and throwing her head back like Mary Tyler Moore used to do.

Sharon admits she got a tremendous sense of success when she started working after she left college. The goal she set for herself was to trade by the time she reached 30. The first time she took the CBOE test she flunked it because she forgot how to calculate fractions. She practiced on cut-up pie and aced it! She has always remembered and acted on her grandmother's advice about the role of failure. "It's an opportunity for learning." Sharon has demonstrated that if you want something bad enough, you can attain it. By 30, she had a badge and was ready for takeoff.

Being sensible, she had an alternative if plan A didn't work out. Plan B: "I was going to Hollywood and star in my own *Roseanne*-like sitcom!" I have no doubt she would have made it with great ratings!

Being a life-affirming positive agent, Sharon gets along well with her colleagues. She is the "crowd rep" whose responsibility it is to explain the "disorganized confusion" by helping groups outside the industry understand it. She likes to be considered "one of the guys" but doesn't think it's necessary to become one. No one threatens her but "don't make me mad." She says, "I make a better friend than an enemy." There are friends on the floor she feels she can call up at three o'clock in the morning if she needs them and they have the same privilege. She feels if a man is a strong figure, he is labeled a success. If a woman is a strong figure, she is labeled a bitch.

Sharon couldn't think of anything or anyone she would find intimidating. Sharon does like to be in control as much as possible. She describes trading as an independent sport but other people need a chance to carry the ball as well. She asks, "Who likes chaos?" She doesn't like it but does have to deal with it and tries rigorously to manage it. "Ignorance is no excuse."

On a competition scale, she calls herself a ten. In addition to sports, she is a ruthless player of games including Trivial Pursuit, Pictionary, and Battleship. She also enjoys a good session of charades and likes to watch boxing on TV.

Friends help her relax. She also tries to find time to spend on her home treadmill to help lose some weight—an occupational hazard as she enjoys cooking and dining out. Favorite vacation spots are Disneyland and Universal Studios.

On a "school night," she's lucky if she makes it past 10:30. She admits she's not a college kid anymore. She's up at 6:00 and out the door. An English muffin and water—no coffee, which tends to make her too wired—see her through the day. By 2:00, she has made or lost enough for the day, and she's gone. Staying longer may just get her in trouble!

In addition to her lapel of lucky pins, Sharon says an occasional prayer. She also ensures good trading by passing through the same turnstile and going up the same elevator to the trading floor. She wouldn't want to assume the risk of following another path! She also takes her jacket home to wash and doesn't like to lose any pins.

Sharon's chapter title, "Lion Trader," came from her description of herself as a lion if she were to choose an animal form. As a Leo, she is playful and fiercely protective. If there is a need, the teeth and claws will come out, an ability especially helpful when she has to take a stand in the market. She relies on experience and her sense of self to negotiate a successful "hunting trip" in the trading fields. Often slow and steady wins over fast and flashy. If you hit, you can score. It's not always necessary to expect a home run or a grand slam. She has observed that very few women traders tend to "bust out," which seems to be more prevalent among the "boys."

Sharon credits many people with providing her the strength her life has required. Heading the list is her grandmother and her two uncles—one a doctor and the other a "Renaissance man." Then there is her foster mom and the priest-coach who is proud of her achievement and plans to send her some mass envelopes for donations to the parish. He taught Sharon that softball is 90 percent mental and 10 percent physical. The same certainly holds true for trading.

Sharon compares the trading arena to school. As in her high school days, there are the class clowns and the kids who think they know everything with everyone interacting. Every day is different. As in school, there is opportunity to have a lot of fun in the pit. The traders are a small group and everyone has a part to play. It sounds like a great source of material should Sharon ever try plan B, the comedy show. The sense of humor that got her the "class clown" label in high school has only improved. She was also most popular and is looking forward to attending a reunion.

The personal quality that she finds really helps is the genuine liking she has for herself. There could be a little less of her; she'd like to lose some weight. She considers herself insightful and a good listener. Sometimes what's needed is a friend who listens and hears, not a therapist. Sharon believes in taking responsibility for herself and everything in her life.

Commenting on the comparison made between trading and war or sex, Sharon said, "If it's war, I'm not taking any prisoners." As for sex, "Not with that group!" She'd rather make money! Getting serious, she described trading as a game. If you go out and play consistently by the rules you set for yourself, you will succeed. You can't expect to win all the time, but you can certainly reach the playoffs!

———————————■———————————

Commenting on the comparison made between trading and war or sex, Sharon said, "If it's war, I'm not taking any prisoners." As for sex, "Not with that group!" She'd rather make money!

————————

Sharon advises prospective traders to be inquisitive, to keep asking questions. No question is too stupid, even if you have to ask it 100 times.

What she really likes about trading are the great hours, the money, and, most of all, the freedom it's given her. If she doesn't feel like going in, she can give herself a day off. That doesn't happen very often. She does have to keep working so she can support her freedom. She's not completely independent financially but is certainly on her way. It's a great feeling for her to be in control of her destiny, especially because in the past so many bad things happened in her life, and all she could do was adapt. Sometimes she feels downright brilliant! She doesn't particularly like the constant air of impending, and often real, catastrophe or occasional jerky and childish behavior as well as the too frequent locker-room atmosphere.

Sometimes Sharon takes a deep breath and reminds herself that she doesn't have to be in on every trade. It can be overwhelming. Like a kid in a candy store, she has learned to pick and choose carefully. You can't have it all. The more frantic you get, the more opportunity for error.

Sharon also observed that she has learned the world is more sexist than racist. She feels quite certain that she could "walk into a Klan meeting and come out with a friend." On the other hand, strong men tend to be perceived quite differently from strong women. She looks forward to the time this perception changes and there's a more even playing field.

She loves her work. "It beats frying chicken!" Sometimes, on a bad day, she tells her colleagues she's heard the McDonald's across the street is hiring. That is usually good for a laugh.

When she barely knew what was going on, one of her friends offered her $50,000 to trade. At the time, she didn't feel qualified to take it. It would have been too risky. Knowing what she does now about managing the risk, the money would be in safe hands. Sharon *does* have a green thumb after all, but it represents her skill as a trader!

# Financial Fishing

## ROBIN MESCH

Prominently displayed on the wall of Robin Mesch's Portland, Oregon, office is a large wooden sign showing a fish about to swallow a hook with the warning, "You'll be sorry if you don't wait for your signal."

Robin believes trading is like fishing. You go out to your favorite spot with your favorite trusty pole, your tackle box of carefully crafted lures, and a few worms to provide protein. You drop your line in the precise spot that you have determined is going to bring you and the fish together and you wait. It takes a great deal of patience. There is constant scanning of ripples, patterns in the water, colors underneath the surface. It is a process of seeing what appears to be impossible to see, what's going on beneath the surface. You are trying to read the fish's, or the market's, "mind" to be in the right place at the right time with the right lure. If it all comes together, you can keep your catch and don't have to return home empty-handed. You don't want to be so hungry or desperate that you end up having worms for dinner!

Of course, trading is much more complex than the description of fishing. I've tried to provide an understandable metaphor for what happens when a trader trades, much like a hunter in pursuit of crafty game or a fisherwoman angling for a wily bass that seems to read her mind. The question is: Which one is going to be caught?

Before this story begins to sound like an article in *Field and Stream,* I want to introduce Robin Mesch, who was either going to be a concert pianist or a trader. These two choices seem quite incompatible and incomprehensible until we understand what each requires of its practitioner. Robin ultimately chose trading, or perhaps trading chose her.

Robin grew up in an upper-middle-class suburb of Cleveland, Ohio, and is the youngest in an all-girl family. She went to Brown University, where she was a religious study major with a semiotic slant. Her major interest, however, was music; she attended a conservatory and performed in a chamber music ensemble. "I was planning on a career as a concert pianist." What happened to divert her from this path that seemed as orderly as the progression of black and white keys?

While she was seriously thinking about what to do in the real world after college, Robin received an offer she couldn't refuse to learn a technical trading method of market analysis. It was her introduction to Drummond geometry, a technical system devised by a Canadian, Charlie Drummond. Almost as eccentric as J. D. Salinger, his technical work is his very own *Catcher in the Rye.* Robin gave it 100 percent, which is the only way she knows once she makes a decision. She views this experience as a turning point in her life.

It was a good match. The journey to understanding the underlying structure and behavior of the markets provided Robin with the intellectual challenge and mental workout on which she thrives. "The more I learned, the more there was to know." It was a journey that ultimately provided an answer to what to do with her life. It has been demonstrated that musicians make excellent traders.

They bring an ability to understand the fundamental frameworks and their changes over time.

———————— ▬▬ ————————

The journey to understanding the underlying structure and behavior of the markets provided Robin with the intellectual challenge and mental workout on which she thrives. "The more I learned, the more there was to know."

————

While she was busy learning the nut and bolts of Drummond's finely tooled system and how to apply them to the intricate and often baffling workings of the market, Robin supported herself by working as a part-time secretary at Harvard Law School. Her parents were under the impression she was headed for the security of graduate school and perhaps a career in law. They didn't understand her total dedication to a new direction and thought she had lost her mind. Although she was working hard to find something, she was viewed as "a lost person who had wandered off the path."

Robin had been smitten by the trading bug. There came a time when she made the ultimate sacrifice, for her, and sold her piano to make ends meet. She didn't get very much for it, but it was what she had to do to keep going. "I just wanted to trade so badly."

The basic Drummond course lasted three years, almost as long as college. It is complex and mysterious and only those deemed worthy of it are invited to learn. Drummond sounds like a financial guru with a cult of followers. "During this early period there was only learning." No "getting behind the wheel"; trading in fact was not allowed until students had graduated and were deemed thoroughly prepared.

"I never doubted that I could master it." She was bright and energetic. Her musical training had accustomed her to recognize patterns and appreciate the role time plays in the behavior of the parts of a pattern. She was also familiar with the concept of flow, which manifests itself in a willingness to fully integrate oneself with an activity in order to achieve maximum results.

In addition, Robin was used to seeking out often overlooked, subtle clues and connections that signal an impending event or anticipate a change in events. Robin brought to trading an already existing complex of discipline, diligence, intellectual rigor, and understanding from her years of dedicated study and musical practice. The market language resembled those dense musical hieroglyphs that required a truly agile and orderly mind to decode.

There is nothing Robin enjoys so much as a problem to solve and a way of reaching a solution through a thorough understanding of all the elements and forces acting on the problem. As she expresses it, "My life has basically been taking that bone and chewing on it." The market provides an enormous mountain of information that resembles a garbage dump to the untrained brain but a virtual treasure trove for those who know what they're looking for and have the means of locating it.

That sounds like a variant of archeology, but it is much more present and future oriented. Drummond geometry, as I understand it, studies the highs and lows of the day's market "tides" and uses that information to predict how much "energy" the market will exhibit on the following day. This sounds quite simple, but it gets very complicated when the dimension of time is entered into the system. As if one time frame weren't enough, Robin works with multiple time frames, following market behavior by using many points of reference.

Drummond geometry builds on previous events. It is a developmental system based on learning. Robin applies this method to her own life, each year hoping to build on what she has learned.

---

Drummond geometry builds on previous events. It is a developmental system based on learning. Robin applies this method to her own life, each year hoping to build on what she has learned.

---

Trading has provided the intellectual challenge Robin had sought in music. In a way it was a journey out, rather than in, connecting her to the stream of information flowing around the world, like rich aortic blood nourishing an organism.

Like her touch on the piano keys, Robin describes her feel for the markets as a "light touch" that suggests sensitivity and the ability to move with dazzling virtuosity. She has a "feel" for the market and can tell if it's going to be an up or down day.

Robin has been applying her skills, not *in* the pit, but *aimed at* the pit as the chief fixed-income technical analyst for Thomson Research, one of the largest providers of proprietary financial research services in the world. She has no problem supporting her statement that her market analysis is highly accurate.

She is also a recognized Drummond expert, a member of a select group, and is qualified to teach its arcane methodology. As if this were not enough, she also writes a newsletter on 30-year bonds. Robin had access to a great mentor, a market Merlin if you will, who provided the guidance, through his system, to help her find her own way. The system is a tool, not the Holy Grail. If it works, use it. There is never a time when Robin stops learning or thinks she knows it all. That would definitely land her in the fish bucket!

Robin faces each day fully prepared, her homework done and armed with a carefully devised plan. "I wait until I see my signal before executing a trade, eliminating as much emotion as possible." If her timing is off, too early or too late, she doesn't blame it on her plan, which is only as good as her execution of it. Don't blame your tennis racket if you miss the ball and lose the game!

Robin does everything she can to micromanage the market. If the market has other plans, she doesn't take it personally. It just means a trip back to the drawing board and being better prepared the next time. She and her partner refer to unexpected market changes as caused by the entrance of Mr. Big! Following market movement also reminded her of driving in Boston, a well-known challenge requiring the ability to ignore false signs and wrong directions and recognize reference points utterly altered by overnight construction. A sense of humor is an important trading asset!

Robin has agonized a great deal over the issue of failure. "Missing an opportunity can turn into a powerful psychological block." Always being alert and quick and studying the hell out of it helps prevent errors of judgment and execution. She is constantly working on bridging the gap between her analysis and its plan-based, signal-triggered execution.

She has no desire to get chewed up in the market's powerful jaws. When she does feel those teeth, she takes time out. "There have been occasions when I have actually lain down on the floor of my office to relax and take stock. One time it got so bad I put a sheet over the computer!" This shroud shielded her from painful information.

As far as market pain is concerned, Robin has developed a very high tolerance. As a day trader, she knows it won't last forever. She is definitely a believer in the philosophy of "no pain, no gain." The market has the power to squeeze tight.

Fear of failure and dealing with it remains a major issue for her and one every trader must confront and learn to handle if he or she is going to have a long-time relationship with the market and not just a one-night stand. "I love being right." Robin does admit she finds being wrong costly and excruciating, especially after all the study and preparation. Trading does force you to come to terms with your own sense of self-worth on a daily basis. Robin tries to keep her ego out of the picture but knows the market has the power to beat her up. She knows she has to avoid that Hamlet-like fear of committing to a course of action and then being responsible for all of the consequences.

Robin does admit to being a control freak, tempered by knowing that she can't expect to control the market, much as she would like to, but she can control her knowledge and how she applies it. She observes that you need those experiences of being wrong so you can become a disciplined trader which is ultimate control. In her estimation, "There is probably no better job for someone like me." Analyzing and determining what is going to happen tomorrow is about as much control as you can expect to exert on the world.

---

Robin does admit to being a control freak, tempered by knowing that she can't expect to control the market, much as she would like to, but she can control her knowledge and how she applies it.

---

One issue that comes up for her is not believing some information she is seeing. It may be something new on the map or something that shouldn't be there. It's necessary to instantly evaluate how much this information, which appears in a field awash with data, is worth. The challenge is to decide what it means and what effect it will have on the market. Her task is to use the market to make money when there is a steady stream, sometimes a gush, sometimes a trickle, of information. "One day I changed my mind so many times, I actually apologized to my broker for calling so many times with seemingly contradictory instructions."

Robin buys time, not price. She is convinced this gives her the best advantage. Time is more powerful. It will force the price to change. She is bringing her multiple time frames into a focus that is totally fluid and dynamic. She describes market forces as a moving amalgam of energy and human nature that she tries to tune into. It's a huge moving medicine ball. Depending on how you play it, the results are positive or negative.

When the outcome is negative and she experiences a substantial loss, she takes a deep breath. Like any other good money manager, she tries to diversify. Other than being better prepared, there is lying down on the floor. She also has been known to do some mind-clearing shopping, usually looking for things for her house.

Laughing is good. On one wall of her office is a picture of big black mountains with a tiny speck. That speck is a fisherman. There is also the fish sign with the warning. Tomorrow is another day.

Robin finds general "life stuff" the best means of unwinding after a draining day. She loves to cook (fish) and an ideal evening is one spent making dinner for her "honey" (who is not in the industry). Not surprisingly, she prefers "comfort food" and leftovers, the older the better! She also makes great stuffed cabbage.

Robin finds meditation helps her work through things, and she tries to keep fit and healthy. She goes to bed between nine and ten and sleeps well until half past four, when her day starts. Robin also finds practicing yoga energizing and a good muscle toner. It's important to collect herself daily for her very demanding work.

Trading has taught her that she can take whatever the market or the world gives, and she can bring her full knowledge and experience to bear on a problem and develop a solution. It's not just about money. Trading has provided her an opportunity for self-mastery that serves as an enormous source of strength and helps her move ahead and continue to develop her skills and understanding. Trading has also made her a technical analysis addict.

Robin feels she has become more solid, more grounded, and more mellow about trading and life. She has gotten a tremendous sense of fulfillment out of trading, allowing her to demonstrate her intellectual powers. There is a great deal of satisfaction in being right. It's a great feeling when she hears the market's music and knows what the next note is. When she is in rhythm with massive market forces, it all comes together.

Robin is highly competitive, and trading has given her an outlet in a field that does not have a lot of winners. She enjoys working with her clients and is glad that she has the luxury of being able to trade off the floor. She has been doing it for 15 years and has no plans to retire. She has survived by being very good at what she does and also having the ability to create a sort of bubble around herself that protects her from the market's sound and fury, helps her focus, and allows her to continue applying fresh research throughout the day. She asks herself, "How can I get this done?" and "How do I get what I want." No matter what, she remains flexible and optimistic and enthusiastic about risk.

Robin also enjoys teaching Drummond geometry to other eager learners. Her advice to anyone interested in pursuing trading as a career is to find the best mentor you can, someone who is genuine and has something of value to teach, and then learn as much as possible. Develop a good plan you believe in because it works and follow it. Try not to sell your piano, but if you do, you'll earn enough trading to buy another one. She feels she was very fortunate in her choice. It is not possible to do it completely on your own. It's too big and complex.

Robin loves the freedom and energy and learning opportunity that trading generates. Where else can you make a decision at half past five in the morning and go home for the rest of the day. Robin is a good illustration of Noel Coward's remark about work, "Work is more fun than fun!" She loves her work and would absolutely do it all over again, piano and all. Incidentally, Robin is thinking about starting piano lessons again!

# CHAPTER 13

# Cash Dance

JANET DISTELDORF

I met Janet Disteldorf on a day when she appeared to have gotten caught in a stampede in the cattle pit at the Chicago Mercantile Exchange (Merc).

As I was to learn, a draining dance or theater rehearsal could also have been the reason for her appearance. We settled down in an empty office at the Merc and began the interview.

Janet is one of the few female traders in the livestock quadrant of the Merc, where futures and options on pork bellies, hogs, cattle, and feeder cattle are traded. Her commodity of choice is cattle, which she has been trading for most of her 15-year career. She began our talk by saying she felt incredibly lucky to have fallen into this area and, of course, to stay successful at it.

Her background certainly gave no clue of her future in futures. Janet grew up in a Chicago suburb in a very close German Catholic family. Her dad is a CPA and her mom a homemaker. Janet changed her major at the University of Illinois at Champagne four times before finally choosing to major in theater and minor in French.

Janet is one of the few female traders in the livestock

quadrant of the Merc, where futures and options on

pork bellies, hogs, cattle, and feeder cattle are traded.

Her commodity of choice is cattle, which she has

been trading for most of her 15-year career.

After graduation, like most people on the outskirts of the arts, Janet needed a day job. An actress friend who was working as a runner at the Merc helped her get a job there. Runners are like the waiters, waitresses, and busboys of the exchanges. They are busy serving and taking orders and doing a lot of work no one else wants to do. Despite this not very attractive job description, they are in an environment where they have an opportunity to learn and be exposed to the workings of a vast industry connected to worldwide economic forces. They fill the spaces between the traders, clerks, and brokers. They are definitely at the entry level, young, and sometimes hungry enough to move up. The path from runner to trader is not a well-worn one. It takes special qualities to make and succeed at that choice.

Janet described herself: "I was an excellent runner. I learned a lot and was constantly asking questions." She worked for a deck holder and remembers that the atmosphere and responsibilities had reminded her of a theater crew working on a production. "I felt right at home and fit into the rhythm."

When she was 25, Janet's grandmother died and left her some money. It wasn't a lot, but it was enough for her to think about using it in a way that would have a maximum benefit for her prospects. She consulted with her CPA dad about the benefits of leasing a seat on the Merc. His advice was that over the long run it was cheaper to buy because prices of seats were always going up. After two and a half years of leasing a seat, Janet decided to go for it. It was like investing in a production that seemed to have a good script and exciting music, but who knew! Janet spent every penny she had and borrowed more money from her dad to make her investment. Janet is someone whose previous purchases had been no bigger than a pair of ballet slippers or a new leotard!

After Janet bought her seat, she went into the forest preserve near her home. She walked and reflected on what she had gotten herself into. There was no way of knowing if she had made the right decision. She would have to do what needed to be done to make it a good choice! It was like a scene straight out of a Broadway musical. A dramatic fork in the road! Janet kept thinking that she "didn't want to end up like a piece of beef on its tines"! She had made a huge commitment, and it was up to her to demonstrate that she had taken the path that would lead her ultimately through and out of the woods.

I'm reminded of the question, "How do you get to Broadway?" The answer is that first you become a star. The missing part is all the behind-the-scenes dedication and hard, purposeful work and talent. Janet did well. "I paid my dad back in a year and a half!"

What helped was her learning ability and desire to be part of the action. She also found a way to use the talents she already possessed. Her vocal training was put to work in projecting and saving her voice. Janet's stage experience made it possible for her to keep a poker face when she was losing money. In retrospect, she looks on the entire experience as theater and realizes the dramatic and exciting quality of the markets is what drew her in.

As a former dancer, "I see the action in the pit and on the floor as pure choreography." Every trader has a set of movements and steps that is integral to the overall production. Some traders are stars and others remain farther from the bright lights. "All that's really missing," Janet continued, "are live cattle wandering around, wondering what all the commotion is about!"

---

As a former dancer, "I see the action in the pit and on the floor as pure choreography." Every trader has a set of movements and steps that is integral to the overall production.

---

Janet admits that trading in the agricultural pits caused her serious stage fright in the beginning. She was scared, even terrified, and found herself trading from a frightened state of mind. This is one of trading's classic no-nos. Fortunately, Janet got rid of the bat-sized butterflies in her stomach before the money and her nerve ran out. She was determined to be part of the "show" and was convinced she could be a standout in this financial production.

What made Janet think she could do it? "I am fiercely independent and was very attracted to the idea of working for myself." She was going to be her own producer, director, star, and even stagehand. There is always something to do in trading that needs her attention. "When you are making money, you can't very well leave. When you are losing money it's definitely no time to leave." You have to stick it out and face those harsh white lights no matter what. Janet has now gotten to the point where she feels confident enough to leave and restore herself in her version of the forest preserve, a house she has built surrounded by the nature she loves. "Deer stray into my backyard, and I have plenty of space to reflect and relax from the turmoil of work."

Janet thrives on facing challenges. She appreciates the fact that every day is different. "You can never know what's going on in the minds of cattle! They can surprise you!" Janet likes being in a situation where she has a say about what she has to do, where she has choices. Mainly, buy-and-sell choices with substantial consequences!

How does Janet prepare for her demanding day? Every morning she begins by listening to ten minutes of the songs of John Melencamp. That clears her mind and serves as a "pumper-upper" for the maniacal frenzy of the trading floor. "It doesn't seem like a lot but it works." She also finds nature is a great decompressor and recharger. She is grateful that she can leave the stress of the day behind and relax in her house in the woods. Janet enjoys reading and had recently reread *East of Eden*. She also likes what she describes as "female fiction." Janet also credits a group of friends, all of whom are in the arts, for helping her not get "puffed up" about what she does.

Janet still loves dancing and also trains and exercises to keep fit and energetic. She also enjoys swimming, which is even more remarkable considering that she has suffered from scoliosis. At the age of 33, Janet's back problems were so severe that she could barely stand up. There are no easy chairs in the pits and it's hard even when you're in perfect health. She underwent surgery and came out of it with steel rods in her back. Even though her occupation would be extremely physically grueling for someone in optimum condition, her physical condition doesn't stop her from being ready to go to work prepared and alert, reminding me of a sports car's ability to accelerate almost instantaneously.

Looking back over her 15-year run, Janet misses "the intimacy and the personal touch of the old pit." The pie has gotten smaller, and she sees the newer traders as more intent on scrambling for their pieces and not connecting with other traders the way the veterans do. Janet reminds me that greed brings out the worst in people. "There is no point in killing yourself or somebody else over money." Janet also perceives the fine line that exists between capitalism and greed and knows which side she feels more comfortable on. So the lesson is not to be too extreme but to maintain a sense of balance.

"There are a couple of traders in the pit who help each other out but mainly it's all up to the individual."

Janet's successes have made her pretty resilient. She doesn't take things as personally as she used to. As she says, "It's hard enough without carrying big chips on your shoulder. They will just weigh you down and distract your focus." The pit has gotten smaller. There is really no place to hide. So it's better to act well. You want to be able to show up the following day and stand next to each other as colleagues.

Janet knows she has earned the high respect of her colleagues whom she describes as "a great group of guys." There is a lot of joking around and she attends their kids' bar mitzvahs and weddings. "Everybody is a character and it's never boring. It's really like show biz!"

Trading has certainly affected her personal life. Janet admits that the only time she doesn't need to be in control is when she is a tourist! On a scale of 1 to 10 measuring competitiveness, she gives herself a 4.

Her boyfriend is not in the financial industry and provides understanding and support after the daily never-ending stress. She agrees with him that the following line from a Billy Joel song is a pretty accurate description of her: "She never gives in . . . she just changes her mind."

Janet has found trading to be a humbling experience that has touched the core of who she is. She is very conscious of the ethics of what she does and is convinced that fair dealers are the only ones who will survive. "I don't take success for granted for a minute" as she mentions a former well-known trader who is now delivering pizzas. Respect plays a major role. "Respecting the spirit of capitalism, respecting your fellow traders, and respecting the market."

Janet has found trading to be a humbling experience that has touched the core of who she is. She is very conscious of the ethics of what she does and is convinced that fair dealers are the only ones who will survive.

Janet believes in keeping cool. When the market gets emotional, it gets irrational. Who knows what causes a stampede. What is important is to avoid getting run over in crowd mentality. "There is no point in being trampled because somebody thought they saw a butterfly. As a wise man said, 'Let's not forget the market is made up out of mere human beings.' "

Janet does not trade or live by any particular rules other than her general observance of ethics already mentioned. Staying disciplined enables her to work her way through the crowd and the cattle dust. "Discipline provides guidance and security when you like trading riskier than the market warrants."

Janet remembers some hectic moments when she was trading the S&P. She also hasn't forgotten getting her brain "fried" during a grueling six-hour session when she was 26. Once is enough! Janet sees these kinds of difficulties as learning experiences. "Trading is definitely a school of hard knocks. The totally out-of-the-blue Chernobyl accident found me short cattle. The lesson I learned is to be prepared; even the most unexpected world event influences a market's behavior."

Janet admits those brain-frying times are extremely difficult to deal with. All you can do is adjust. It is crucial to get rid of the overwhelming stress that can be so incapacitating. Janet knows to limit her losses, put on a Band-Aid and wait for the "barrel to stop turning."

Janet describes herself as "not very materialistic." With a dad and a brother who are CPAs, she tends to be financially conservative and doesn't buy a car unless she can pay cash for it. Her major purchase since buying her seat is a getaway house. Janet's idea of money well spent is traveling because she feels it's a great mind clearer. She has gone hiking and biking all over Europe and has visited the Caribbean islands. Africa remains on her list of places to see.

Janet is very generous with her family. Not having children of her own, she especially enjoys doing things for the children of her siblings. She can always be relied on to come through for ballet lessons or whatever else is needed and has taken her niece with her to Europe. Janet fully appreciates the benefits her career has given her. She can take two months off if she wants to. "The money is the means of keeping score. The real value is in having the ultimate freedom to be able to do what I enjoy."

When asked to come up with an image of the market and her relationship to it, Janet described it as a mountain. "A mountain which only lets me get so far up its slopes." She is always in a position of starting again and trying to get just a little farther than before. She sees herself engaged in a constant struggle, whether it's going well or badly. As long as she knows she has to go up that mountain again, it's hard to relax.

Janet is always aware of that little reminder in the back of her mind that doesn't let go and probably helps her keep her edge. "It can be an effort to make the effort." The same gritty qualities that enabled her to go to auditions and handle rejections come into play on the floor. "The market knocks you down. You get yourself back up and keep going." Many times it's sheer will power. Janet is small and does not project a particularly tough image, but there is definite strength and passion.

Trading is a psychological as well as a physical struggle. Janet doesn't get intimidated the way she did when she started. People do try and she sees a lot of game playing, a lot of egos thrown around. She says, "I've been there too long and have pretty much seen it all." The physicality can get out of hand at times. The closes can get very rough, and there have been occasions when she has found herself literally sitting on the floor. Her parents have never seen her trade, and she thinks they would be astonished if they did.

Janet credits her family as the well of her strength. She describes her upbringing as "incredibly solid." She is very close to her family and says she is who she is. There are people down there, and elsewhere, who are their money. That is not for her.

Five years ago she could get by on scalping. Now she is a position trader and studies charts for buy-and-sell points. With the introduction of computerized trading, Janet feels it's not worth fighting for every tick. Other than that, she doesn't follow any particular methodology and usually doesn't have a market opinion.

What Janet does follow is her intuition, which she describes as "incredibly reliable." If she doesn't listen to it, she usually regrets it. Janet reports that 90 percent of the time when she is following her instincts, she is making money. That is an excellent return! On the other hand, she does admit that it's difficult to trust her intuition when she's losing. "It's not easy to get back in the saddle after you've taken a spill or your "horse" (in her case a 1,200- to 1,400-pound steer) has rolled over on you."

Janet would not describe herself as superstitious but she does retire any jewelry she was wearing on a day that has turned out to be bad to a "bad luck" drawer, where it remains. Fortunately, this is a very small drawer, and that's the way she wants to keep it.

If she ever tired of struggling up the mountain, Janet would like to do something with her background in French. She is very patient and can see herself teaching. The theater still draws her, but there it would have to be something that didn't require dancing because of her back problems.

Where male traders have often described trading in terms of sex or war, Janet, interestingly but hardly surprisingly, sees it as a dance. She says, "I can read its choreography, which enables me to enter the market's rhythm." Trading is a puzzle that Janet continues to find challenging. "On good days, it's an opportunity for problem solving. On bad days, it resembles rolling blindly in a barrel!"

If this sounds appealing, she advises following her path and learning from the bottom up as a runner. That way you know the good, the bad, and the ugly, and you can decide if you have what it takes to take on the mountain. Janet recommends getting a sense of the rhythm of the floor. Otherwise, it's going to appear like dissonance, and you'll never know where to make your move and play your part. Clerking for a trader is a great way to learn. Their stress becomes your stress even though it's not coming out of your pocket. If she had a daughter who was temperamentally suited for trading, she would encourage her to go for it.

It's necessary to have exposure to risk and learn how to deal with it. Janet is of the opinion that "it's easier for a stupid guy to make money than a smart woman." The men have their network and many are former athletes. Janet feels that as a woman she needs to be smarter and faster to compete. The trading floor is not even. As long as she is aware of that fact, she can design her dance accordingly to take it into account. The loss of the agility of youth is balanced by experience-based strategy.

The older traders know what they're doing while the younger, newer, more insecure men feel they have to prove themselves by going for the home run. Janet feels she has found her niche in this theater—the trading floor—and the drama plays out on an always shaky mountainous terrain. No matter what unexpected conditions she finds herself in, Janet always gets her trade. Despite market swings and those occasional frightening rolls in the barrel, she always gets home and lands on her feet. Janet sees herself more as the turtle than the hare. Slow but steady and consistent with her mind's eye on the goal.

Her career trading has given her freedom, a good living, and self-respect. In her words, "You know who you are. You are defined by something." Much of it is about people, and she has enjoyed the camaraderie that trading has provided. She is definitely part of the ensemble.

Janet thinks her ability to remain down-to-earth has been the quality that has served her best. It has kept her grounded and protected her from the occupational hazard of "puffing up." She sees herself as resilient, hardworking, and honest but feels she is not as disciplined, ambitious, or aggressive as she could be. "I could be making more money if I were challenged by a goal other than just the money." But she adds, "I don't have to worry about my blood pressure and I can enjoy watching the deer in my backyard."

Janet has found trading fun even on bad days. She continues to enjoy her work, saying "nothing is for nothing." She loves what she does and considers that she is fortunate in having the ultimate freedom of doing what she likes and is good at.

Other than appreciating her work more and taking it less for granted, there is nothing she would change if she had it to do all over again. Janet would be eager once more to join the dance.

# CHAPTER 14

# A Woman for All Seasons

## MEI PING YANG

Mei Ping's name in Chinese translates as "screen of plum blossoms." The underlying meaning is strength. Plum blossoms are hardy blooms that are known to appear before the start of spring, considerably ahead of other signs of resurgent life and energy. Her parents' choice of this particular name out of the thousands of possibilities couldn't have been more appropriate. She is incredibly strong, although she *seems* fragile as a plum blossom should. The element of the screen adds additional protection and also mystery. Her name is apt on another level as Mei Ping has chosen to trade foreign currencies from a computer screen—the closest thing to pit trading there is without being there. The advantages are relative peace and quiet, as well as ease because you can sit back and put your feet up. In Mei Ping's case, "Because I actively spread many currencies and in addition handled investment management, it would have been virtually impossible for me to operate inside a trading pit." For someone as self-contained as Mei Ping, her trading reached out in many directions at a furious and determined pace. Think of it as a game of chess with the pieces representing the constantly fluctuating values based on the economic health of individual countries.

The complexity that Mei Ping has maneuvered around with such intellectual agility is nothing short of astounding. It is one thing to become expert in one currency or even two, but she has been able to keep multiple strands straight and productive. It's like a tapestry of many colors and threads. If that were not sufficiently challenging, keep in mind that the colors as well as the numbers and quality of the threads are constantly changing. In addition, these changes influence the rest upward or downward as we'll see. It takes a unique individual to be attracted to this field and be successful in it.

Mei Ping has already been mentioned in several books. As vice president of proprietary foreign exchange trading at a major firm, she spent two intense Wall Street years trading currencies worldwide. On a daily basis, she was required to research, respond to, and anticipate what was going on with the lifeblood of the world's economies. Much like a blood workup, she had to evaluate the meaning of the levels and their relationships to each other. She was responsible for putting to work hundreds of millions of dollars, basing her decisions on fluctuations in a variety of foreign currencies. There are times when it must be like trying to follow the whims and ways of a giant baby. Is the baby going to lurch forward or backward, sit down on the floor, or throw a tantrum? Money is as integral to our lives as the air we breathe and the blood that travels through our circulatory system. Indeed, it is the substance that courses through all the world's veins and arteries, nourishing the entire organism. At times, there are episodes of anemia or, on the other hand, overly rich blood with its attendant consequences. Some areas seem to have better-stocked "blood" banks than others. At times, there is an urgent need for a transfusion. Occasionally, the patient can't be saved!

Mei Ping has been like a highly skilled technician analyzing the substance of currency trading in all its mutations from country to country. It is a major means of global communication connecting individuals, people, nations, and areas.

Mei Ping first became aware of the global dimension of currency trading when she watched a meeting of the United Nations Assembly on the black-and-white screen of a little portable Sony, a gift from an uncle. Mei Ping was a young child at the time, but this experience made an indelible impression. Her next memory of an event that contributed to her career choice was seeing the modern classic play *A Man for All Seasons*, which tells the story of the archbishop of Canterbury, Sir Thomas More, whose wide range of interests dramatized qualities she saw in herself. She felt she shared his perspective of events and their consequences.

Mei Ping was born in Singapore but her family lived in Malaysia for ten years as refugees from communist China. She thus experienced a diversity of cultural and economic systems before returning to her birthplace. She is an intensely private and self-contained person and didn't have much to say about the early phase of her life other than the memory of being discriminated against in Malaysia for her being Chinese. She also remembers being happy. Once! Mei Ping has a well-developed sense of humor that she doesn't keep in a drawer.

Her father is a merchant and her mother remains an artist working in traditional Chinese porcelain painting characterized by patient work with an economy of marks. She remembers her mother always keeping up with news of the larger world.

Mei Ping majored in finance in college but also studied history, which has continued to be an interest. A graduate-level international finance course put the idea of currency trading in her head and there it remained. Her first job was at the Singapore branch of a substantial Norwegian bank. She was fortunate in working under someone who clearly recognized her talent and potential, and allowed her to take calculated risks. Mei Ping was able to trade under the aegis of this individual while learning the ropes. "I was very fortunate to have had an experience with someone who allowed me to learn." Mei Ping described herself as "ready to learn." She puts tremendous emphasis on learning and intelligent action and loves teaching. She is true to her name for plum blossoms are eager to make their move and tend not to wait for spring with the rest of the crowd. Her interest in learning can sometimes be misperceived, not really understood. It should not be read as selfishness or a lack of sociability but as a complete dedication to studying the entire text to be able to respond intelligently and effectively.

---

She is true to her name for plum blossoms are eager to make their move and tend not to wait for spring with the rest of the crowd.

---

The apprentice-mentor relationship Mei Ping had at the Norwegian bank was an ideal learning opportunity, and she made the most of it. At the same time it was very difficult because she was left alone to make mistakes. "It can be a very frightening experience." This was at a time when the Asian markets were entering a period of tremendous growth and expansion. Her experience in cross-country currency trading put her in a unique position to play an active role in this newly energized and potentially huge market.

Mei Ping determined right away that she could do it. She found trading fascinating and intellectually challenging. As with the United Nations and *Man for All Seasons*, it was a highly dramatic activity. Things happened! There were important interactions that caused a chain reaction of events in multiple directions and areas. Mei Ping practiced testing an idea with pencil and paper, putting it through its paces, sketching it out like an artist. She learned not to be afraid of being wrong. "The whole point was to learn from each event so it was not a lesson lost."

Mei Ping was constantly engaged in refining her trading ideas. She reminded me how easy it is to be discouraged, how easy it is to give up or not even try. She does admit she is endowed with serious stick-to-it-ivness as well as its evil twin, stubbornness, which can produce inflexibility at times when she is convinced she is right. Mei Ping learned control from watching her mother's patient skill with brush and paint. The end result is a formulation of a firm, but flexible, plan that takes into account the complexities of one or several or multiple currencies as they play off each other. Currency is consumed much like a grain or a piece of meat. A country's economic state produces this paper "crop." It may seem fragile but it has tremendous potential in the realm of world power.

To Mei Ping the currency markets are as familiar as *Personal Choice,* a favorite BBC radio show based on the music preferences of individuals. An important feature of this program is making unexpected connections, tying together bits and pieces that seem to have no relationship to each other. It is worth noting the words *personal choice* and to keep in mind that Mei Ping chose trading. She was initially exposed to trading on a philosophical level and right away knew this was something she could and should do. She was inclined to give it her all in order to learn. There may have been some sense of the underlying security of a nation's wealth that gave her confidence. It appears that on some level Mei Ping was convinced that her involvement as an expert would prevent the type of politically produced, unexpected displacement that she experienced as a child.

Mei Ping set out to become fluent in currencies and in their language and relationship with each other. When it came to trading, she felt she was going to be able to do it because "when push came to shove, I had always been able to do it internally." Mei Ping already knew she could rely on herself. Whatever she set out to do would happen. Her strong mother remains a major influence on her character as well as her life. Her mother always told Mei Ping that being a girl shouldn't prevent her from accomplishing whatever she set out to do despite the traditional Chinese practice of favoring male children. The other basic life lesson she learned from her mother was that tomorrow is another day. Mei Ping believes it's important to keep changing. "Those who don't, write their own death sentence." Her family and her upbringing are the wells from which her strength flows.

Mei Ping has found through her research-based work that she is much more persistent than she thought she was. To say it in her words: "I would make a good bee!" Bees have the ability to concentrate on the task at hand and keep working until it's completed. "Let's not forget all this visiting of flowers is work, not frivolity!"

---

"I would make a good bee!" Bees have the ability to

concentrate on the task at hand and keep working

until it's completed.

---

Another one of her essential qualities is her love of learning. She has what she termed a scholarly approach to analyzing a problem and working out a solution. "I believe in the value of keeping an open mind." She says people sometimes misinterpret her openness and tolerance for other viewpoints and her willingness to consider the ideas of others as a lack of certainty. Nothing could be further from the truth. She believes that if something is interesting, that's justification enough for wanting to add it to her mental files. Mei Ping has strong convictions supported by solidly researched reasoning.

Mei Ping has also been strengthened by the fact that she is spiritually grounded. Although she doesn't follow an organized religion, she does reflect on what is going on in her life. Mei Ping also regards her friends as a valuable bulwark against self-doubt.

She considers her trading as a journey into herself. She has constantly had to ask herself if she was being honest with herself, honest in what she had done. "In the end, it is necessary to answer to yourself. No one else can really know what you're doing the way you do. The question to ask yourself is would you want yourself as a customer? Are you producing a product you would want to use?"

Integrity is an uppermost priority for Mei Ping. She has to feel totally comfortable with what she is doing. As she said, "If you find a comfortable home, move in." Despite her high-level, stress-laden trading career, she has made it comfortable for herself because she has always been able to return to herself. It is very important not to lose yourself as you delve into the arduous study of market behavior.

Remembering a particular incident that stood out in her memory, Mei Ping said that when she was testing an idea early in her trading days, she found particularly fascinating what would happen when money was put into the mix. It was at this point that the validity of her idea was tested. Although it at first appeared not to be working as she had predicted and her body temperature kept changing from hot to cold, she held on. The afternoon opening of the London markets proved her idea correct; her research had been valid, and she made back all the money she was afraid she was in danger of losing. "It is necessary to believe in yourself and your abilities if you've done the required work that provides the psychological backup."

Mei Ping's worst moments have been those when she didn't stick to her guns and give her ideas a chance to flower. Another danger is in wanting to please everyone all the time. "If it's a fundamentally good and carefully researched plan, following it will bring a successful result. The research and knowledge need to be so excellent that it is possible to have faith in it and believe in yourself and your ability to carry it out."

"Losses or a losing streak does occur. The proper response is to be better prepared, return to research, and improve your per-formance. It's necessary to return to the research and to work on the basic idea that is manifested as the plan. It is not easy and requires coping skills."

As Mei Ping has traded from a computer screen, she has not had to deal with the daily "Seinfeldisms" of the pit, but she does admit that life can get complicated. She advises against gossiping, which has a tendency to wander away from truth. Mei Ping is open to other views even though she finds it gratifying that she is usually right. She quoted an old wise man: "If you convince a man against his will, he is of the same opinion still. "

She continues to refine her ideas and would like to be more adept at "calling the punches." She is a quick learner who reminds herself to pay attention to her lessons, to be more patient, and to have less of a tin ear so she can hear what the market is saying in its many voices. The screen removes her from the sweat of the market and allows her to interact on a slightly more peaceful level.

Describing her relationship to the market, Mei Ping sees it as a "very bad spouse on occasion." The problem is basically one of communication where one side doesn't understand the other. "To make the relationship function, there has to be correct under-standing." The major difficulty in maintaining a successful relation-ship with the market is that often there isn't time to achieve this ideal state of understanding; but it does help to be aware of it.

What does Mei Ping look for in her research? She applies her scholarly methods and reads, reads, and reads, looking for patterns that support an idea she has about the market. It is as tricky as going out on a date with someone who is not giving straight information and says no when he really means yes. There is a lot of reading between the lines involved in the complex process of market study.

Describing her relationship to the market, Mei Ping sees it as a "very bad spouse on occasion." The problem is basically one of communication where one side doesn't understand the other.

Mei Ping recommends sticking with a good plan, staying honest, and keeping the system running. The organism needs to be tended and kept alive. Mei Ping starts with a simple model of what she sees and is then always tinkering with it, trying to improve it with each new bit of information that comes in. It is like feeding information to see how the model likes it. Does it accept the offering or ignore, or even reject, it?

Mei Ping's kind of trading can be very isolating but has suited her more solitary style. She is somewhat like the person in the projection booth running images through light to build an integrated whole on the screen. Although the heat of the pit is missing, she generates her own fire. It's internal and is fueled by the danger of making the wrong decision. Mei Ping's challenge is to work with herself, to talk to herself. Her task is to constantly reinvent herself , to be the right person to meet the most recent market demand. To be the best match for the job. She prides herself on being resourceful and is disappointed in herself when she doesn't rise to the demands of the market moment. Mei Ping recalled one time when she wasn't resourceful and it really affected her personal life to the degree that she had to take several months off to renew herself. There is no point in beating up on yourself and that is one invitation she doesn't accept. Mei Ping tries to heed her mother's advice: "Why defeat yourself before you begin?"

She describes herself as highly competitive, but she is competing against herself, her last research, or her last effort. Mei Ping is very hard on herself. She has extremely high standards that she expects herself to meet and even exceed. Despite her high-pressure work, she thinks of herself as very easygoing and has developed an incredible resiliency. She believes in putting the past behind her where it belongs and moving forward.

For a diversion, she enjoys playing computer games, even those she describes as silly such as "Minesweeper." She is attracted by what needs to happen to be able to continue the game, which is a definite parallel to trading. You want to stay in the game and not suffer shutdown or get the "game is over" message. She is a serious believer in, and student of, game theory as well as chaos theory, virtually anything that will help her in her work. Mei Ping admits that she does have a tendency to research something to death and has been known to get obsessed with an idea.

Mei Ping could do a lot of different things other than trading. She has a first-rate analytical mind that finds many areas interesting. "A major problem is lack of time." Basically, any discipline that gives her an opportunity to learn is a good match. Although she is a superb learner, she has never really been called on to teach anyone else and might like to try that. She has a huge body of ideas to share and an ability to throw all her energy at a problem. Mei Ping has a lot of joie de vivre for her work, particularly its learning aspects. She does believe in doing what you do with dedication and love.

Listening to great music relaxes her after a demanding day. She prefers the pure happiness and spirituality of Gregorian chants as well as other medieval music. Mei Ping also likes a good laugh and says she only dares to be funny with people she knows quite well. Her sense of humor is situational and her brand of humor intelligent. She misses her favorite radio show, the BBC's *Personal Choice*, which presents eccentric and improbable situations dealing with individuals and their work. It is the kind of very simple but effective humor that the English have developed into a high art.

Does Mei Ping find trading fun? "There are moments when it is exquisite and moments when it is painful. There have been times when I couldn't do anything wrong and other times when I couldn't get anything right." Overall, the positive times are the result of understanding. She has learned that the easy answer is very often not the best answer and is irritated by the rush to success at any cost. Those times when she has hit all the spots right have been enormously satisfying.

Mei Ping admits trading can be very exciting if you are in a charged positive state of mind. She would ask those contemplating trading as a career choice whether they realize what they were getting into. If the answer is yes, she advises exploring the possibilities. Mei Ping also recommends having "a handy exit as you might get more than you bargained for." What she really respects about her work is that it is impersonal: The market doesn't have a personal vendetta against her nor is it arbitrary. She finds that it's very democratic and very fair. "It can be equally frustrating or gratifying."

Mei Ping has gotten a great deal of enjoyment from the process of doing her demanding work. There have been very good financial rewards. Enjoyment of her work has been very important and, in keeping with her personal policy of openness, she is willing to explore other challenges. She does not restrict herself to the traditional lifetime career position. Mei Ping is in the process of returning to investment management because she prefers the much more strategic analysis of the markets associated with equities and bonds. She remains interested in the macropolicy aspects of decision making with their global consequences.

Mei Ping was not sure she would necessarily do it all over again. Although she has been tremendously successful and has developed high-level specialized skills, she would also be happy as a historian focusing on central Asia, studying the "screen" of history for clues and patterns in ancient as well as new trade routes.

# CHAPTER 15

# The Physics
of Trading

ROSLYN ABELL

I met Roslyn Abell on a clear fall afternoon in her spacious apartment that is actually two apartments combined, like a his and hers, overlooking the Chicago Yacht Club and Lake Michigan. Our trader husbands are partners and have collaborated on several books about trading as well as having written on their own. Although she no longer trades, I knew Roslyn had a long trading career and had been extremely successful at it, as she is at anything she sets her mind to. For a while Roslyn and Howard were a trading couple. She is a highly intelligent, down-to-earth, and energetic woman with a quick mind, and she is happiest when challenged and actively pursuing complex ideas. We took a look at the last boats of fall catching the breeze on the lake and then got started.

Roslyn's first taste of trading was in the potato market in the late sixties. As a market analyst for Bache, which was subsequently absorbed by Prudential, she was responsible for writing daily commentaries on potatoes as well as pork bellies, sugar, soy beans, wheat, and corn. This was her introduction to the discipline of charts and suited her mathematical background. Roslyn observed, "I became director of commodity research for the midwest region at E. F. Hutton just at the time when commodity markets were getting ready to take off." What path had Roslyn taken to arrive at this interesting point in the commodity business? It certainly wasn't a straight one by any means.

Roslyn's parents were Russian Jewish immigrants who had settled in Brooklyn. Her father, a plumber and heating contractor, was educated in his native language and felt more comfortable working with numbers than with the more-difficult-to-pronounce English words. He communicated his feeling for numbers at Roslyn's bedtime when, instead of reading her stories, Roslyn was encouraged to add, subtract, divide, and multiply in her head. She also learned numbers stories. "Numbers were fun and I could do interesting things with them."

The appeal of numbers for both father and daughter was that they were real and could be put to work to solve problems and could be found everywhere in actual life. Roslyn and her brother experienced the importance of numbers firsthand. They both earned a living at an early age. There was always work to be done around their father's shop. Early on, Roslyn was exposed to the practical use of science in daily life.

Roslyn was good-natured and did whatever was required. Although her teachers would have preferred that she devote herself to her schoolwork full-time, at 16 she received her working papers and got a job at the candy counter of a neighborhood movie theater. The result of that career move didn't turn out to be "historical," although a movie connection has recently emerged in her life.

College was not in the picture that Roslyn's parents had for her future. Although she had failed a typing course, they saw her following in the secretarial footsteps of her cousins. But they had not reckoned with Roslyn! All those bedtime sessions with numbers had left their mark. Science was what she chose for herself. After all, she had practical experience. Whenever her mother left Roslyn with her older brother, Roslyn was always pursuing scientific knowledge. Her laboratory was the bathroom and her chemicals of choice, by necessity, were whatever she could reach and open. She remembers complex compounds and mixtures whose secret ingredient was often nail polish remover. "You work with what you have!" Another interest, incorporating basic chemistry, was cooking. At nine she was preparing family meals. She still views cooking as domestic chemistry and physics that illustrate laws of thermodynamics and energy transfer. No wonder she enjoys it so much!

Needless to say, Roslyn did not go on to the secretarial pool but was accepted at the University of Rhode Island, where she began studying chemistry. She subsequently transferred to Brooklyn College, closer to home, and also switched her major from chemistry to economics, being one of the few women in her classes.

Roslyn found a position as a price reporter at a Wall Street company. It was her introduction to commodities and she was hooked. "I could use my skills and also apply and expand what I had learned about economics. My job was to analyze and research various commodity trends." She found the work and the atmosphere very exciting, and it beat typing by quantum leaps.

Roslyn advanced to account executive and worked with farmers and ranchers who had their own ideas about the value of what they produced. She had good sales ability and a strong sense of responsibility for her clients, who did well.

"This was a time when it was possible for an independent operator to become very wealthy." She met legendary trader George Segal at Bache and later they both worked at E. F. Hutton, where she helped him set up his futures operation. Roslyn introduced George to futures the way mothers teach their children about sex. George took to it in a big way. She also learned a great deal from this association, which she was later to put to work trading on the floor.

What made Roslyn think this was the right direction for her? Roslyn is the kind of person who, when she decides she is going to do something, does it! She felt very much at home with the technical aspects of trading, such as the mathematical systems and technical charts. She put her hard earnings to work, and it was not money she was going to lose!

---

Roslyn found out when she began studying physics that she was using a fundamental Newtonian law of physics and applying it to commodities.

---

Roslyn gradually refined her trading—"I developed a trading system that my husband uses to this day." Interestingly, Roslyn found out when she began studying physics that she was using a fundamental Newtonian law of physics and applying it to commodities. It is designed to tell what price closes keep momentum going in the same direction. Little did Newton realize what future applications his observations would have!

---

Little did Newton realize what future applications his observations would have!

---

The other physical theory that Roslyn used, realizing it only later when she was working on her degree in physics, is that of quantum mechanics, which she uses to describe a price level. The way it works is that electrons change energy levels as they move among different "shelves," much as a cat jumps from a lower shelf to a higher one. An energetic electron can travel farther than a low-energy, "tired" electron. The energy, or price, is the value of the electron, or commodity.

Roslyn creates her own challenges. She has found that the more difficult path leads to the more interesting place. Life is short. There is a great deal to do and she is committed to enjoying life by doing, not by lounging around.

Roslyn observes, "I am extremely competitive but mainly with myself." She is always pushing herself to exceed her last accomplishment. Roslyn works on reaching one set of goals and then moving on to another. She is probably one of the least complacent people I know. Even though she has a background in trading and a degree in economics and one in physics, she has launched into a new area—film production—as a way of learning a business that combines two of her loves, art and science. In addition, she is working on writing a mystery novel with a female protagonist.

ROK, as her badge symbol indicated, learned to trade by studying charts and reading books on chart trading. Roslyn recalled, "I couldn't have picked a better mentor than David Johnston and would have worked for him for nothing." As his assistant at Hutton, she had a priceless opportunity to learn his trading methods and opinions. She also learned to keep her cool, not to panic, and, most important of all, to always ask Is this real or isn't it? to distinguish the genuine from the phantom. Roslyn increased her store of technical methods and knowledge from this renowned financial fundamentalist. Roslyn remembers seeing lines on his charts that she had never seen before and wondering what they meant. She was learning a new language, the language of trading with its grammar composed of numbers and vectors instead of letters.

Roslyn has even more vivid recollections of her work relationship with innovator David Johnston during her time at E. F. Hutton. She was the only woman in her position. The morning would begin with a discussion with David on his trading plans for his clients if prices reached certain levels. Later in the day, he would "get my attention to act on the morning's discussions either by banging on the desk or gesturing animatedly with his hands!" It was like morning rounds with the chief surgeon. Roslyn learned that it's advisable to put aside your ego when you are learning from someone whose ideas you respect. It is a time to learn, according to her, and to incorporate something of value into your method, if you have one. "Save the competition for later when you are on your own." Roslyn believes women tend to be more patient. As a result of this experience, she was even more determined to become an independent trader.

Leaving home for the first time to go away to college in Rhode Island had been a defining experience. Roslyn found out that she had the courage of her convictions, was fervently independent, scrupulously responsible, and immune to peer pressure. The association with David Johnston was another pivotal event. Roslyn adds that "the birth and raising of my son Alex was transformational."

She also found time to earn a long-desired degree in physics at the University of Illinois, where there was some very exciting high-energy physics research being conducted that involved identification of the "top quark," one of the six prime elements of all matter. Earning this degree was a way for Roslyn to demonstrate to herself that her mental ability remained first-rate. Chemistry courses were no problem as she had to do what she had done earlier as a young child experimenting with "bathroom chemistry." Later, when she returned to school, Roslyn was attracted by the ability of physics to explain so much. In addition to pulling a straight "A" average in her last two years, Roslyn was the only undergraduate on the D-zero project at Fermi Lab. She credits her son with helping her return to the learning track and revitalizing her rusty study habits.

Roslyn prepared for the demanding trading day by staying fit and energetic. She continues to enjoy a wide variety of sports, including running, swimming, and judo as well as sailing and aerobics! She also has a punching bag, the real thing, hanging in a large room in her home that is dedicated to fitness. Roslyn admits there is a lot of aggression stored up during the trading day that needs to be released. You can't hit the guys or strike back at the market after it delivers an unforeseen blow. The punching bag helps! She also used to engage in target practice at the old gun club on Lake Michigan!

Roslyn feels that playing challenging games such as chess is a good stress reducer. Travel also provided great time-out from trading, and the family used to make regular trips to Florida and to Hawaii as well as Europe. Roslyn's son could always be relied on to get his parents' trading-fevered minds cooled down and focused on what was really important—playing with a young boy! Roslyn never allowed herself to be a victim and handled making and losing money with an equal sense of balance.

"I traded it but didn't live it." By that she means that she and her husband didn't need ostentatious displays of wealth to indicate their status in the world. They have a good sense of who they are. Trading had a positive effect on their life. In addition to providing a good living, it provided the flexible hours and freedom to spend a lot of time with their son. "The trading pits do have good employee benefits!"

The personal qualities that helped her trade are a healthy aggressive drive tempered by her very logical mind. Roslyn is also someone who is visually oriented and has highly developed conceptualizing skills. Another contributing attribute has been her love of learning. A major factor has been the empathetic working relationship she has enjoyed with her husband—a man with a unique understanding of his wife. Instead of a vacation house or some luxury item, he gave Roslyn her brain's desire, the freedom to return to school and earn a physics degree. As a commodities couple, they traded conservatively, using her system to produce results. It was virtually an ideal situation. Trading totally validated her sense of independence. The experience also gave her an opportunity to deal honestly and fairly, as she likes to do. She and her husband both earned their seats and she felt she always treated hers with care and respect. It is not like other jobs. It's fast, it's risky, it's demanding but it's worth every tick.

Roslyn is not easily intimidated and could only recall one incident in her life when she felt she clearly lost her usual cool. The actor Cary Grant was doing a commercial upstairs from E. F. Hutton and came down to sign autographs. The one and only time she has lost her power of speech, as her husband will attest, was when she was shaking hands with the matinee idol.

Roslyn thinks of herself as courageous and not afraid to live or work. She gets her strength from her parents, who instilled the work ethic in her at a young age. "Self-esteem follows from doing well at something worth doing."

Like physicists Newton and Einstein, Roslyn prefers simple but comprehensive rules with wide application. Her favorite for trading as well as life: "Don't waste my time!" This is someone who is always busy doing something productive. Her attitude is that there is so much to learn, so why stand around waiting for apples to strike you on the head. This is a woman who loves to learn and is happiest, as she has been since an early age, learning something that is challenging and real.

Her best moments—those she finds most satisfying—are characterized by the exchange of something real. It can be love or it can be information. If you want to put a smile on Roslyn's face, present her with a problem to solve!

Roslyn's list of problem areas is a short one. She is a very confident woman who likes to speak her mind, literally. She admits this tendency to be outspoken has occasionally embarrassed her low-key husband. An area in which she does not do well is dealing with death, which makes her feel totally helpless. One of the few things she ever wanted to do well and did not succeed in was ice skating. "I do better with friction."

As for handling trading losses, Roslyn is an extremely adaptable and positive woman with considerable inner resources and a unique sense of ironic humor. She remembers one occasion in particular when she and husband Howard had taken a severe beating in the market. Her response was to get her husband and son dressed up and out to dinner at the expensive Maxim's of Paris. The intention was to make everyone feel better and remember that life is to be enjoyed. It lifted their spirits and certainly motivated them to return to the pit the following day in order to pay for the meal!

Roslyn's preference for simple but solid extends to her concept of success. It is hardly surprising that she does not judge it in furs, cars, or jewelry. Anytime you get more than you bargained for is good. A successful day is one in which you have found something to laugh about or smile at . . . as well as one on which you get to keep your money!

---

Roslyn's preference for simple but solid extends to her concept of success. It is hardly surprising that she does not judge it in furs, cars, or jewelry.

---

She always enjoyed excellent rapport with her colleagues, whether traders or physicists. Throughout her career, she was accustomed to the society of men and has preferred spending time and working with individuals who, like herself, are actively engaged in exploring and appreciating life.

Roslyn sees similarities between the scientific laboratory and the trading "laboratory." In both settings ideas are being tested and put through their rigorous paces. Scrupulous measurements are taken and acted on. Variables are introduced. Results are carefully studied and used as a source of information for the continuing research-based market exploration.

Roslyn points out an interesting parallel between trading and physics. She sees both as concerned with energy. Roslyn describes each commodity as having its own unique signature rhythm. Corn to her moves to a definite waltz tempo. Soybean behavior suggests rock and roll or Beethoven! There is no question that wheat demonstrates a country-and-western predilection. Bellies move to a nameless strong beat. In other words, each commodity moves to the sound of its own drummer. Currencies resemble percussion instruments.

This description gives a graphic sense of the tremendous energy and vitality of that ceaseless hive of human industry, the world's marketplace. It is possible to sense its complex chemical and physical properties. I can't help but think that lots of people just trade, unaware that what they are wearing are not trading jackets but lab coats!

Expanding the music metaphor, Roslyn sees the entire trading system as a symphony orchestra with interconnected individuals using talent and skill to contribute to the excellence of the entire enterprise. Winning or "running hot" allows you to participate successfully; losing means you're out, you're not on the same page on the right note. You are "running cold" and out of tune with the market's performance. It's time to stop trading and find your place and get into the right rhythm. There is little point in humming "Moon Over Miami" when everyone else is working through "Rites of Spring"!

Roslyn recalled an experience in a different context that helps to describe the feeling of finding the right tune in the noise of the market. She had gone to Puerto Rico on holiday and, as a nongambler, was enjoying the proverbial beginner's luck at the casino tables. "I could do no wrong. The chemistry and physics were right. It all meshed to make the moment work." The "tune" was right.

In the market, doing the right thing at the right time in the right place is by no means accidental. It's a result of painstaking study of the system that Roslyn developed to see what it will do with fresh data. Roslyn recalled fondly the bull markets in grains in the seventies. Her system has proven to be a reliable, adaptable, smooth-running vehicle no matter what data she feeds it. She just has to be alert to its signals.

Roslyn feels she would be suited to any field in which she would call on her analytical ability and skill at conceptualizing ideas. Besides being able to work as part of a team to complete a project, she can point to a solid history of expert business operation and administration and the indispensable problem-solving skill. Roslyn is a highly intelligent and resourceful person with practical experience that can transfer into new areas. She observed "A think tank would be ideal!"

Roslyn thinks commodities trading is a great career for a woman, especially if she is contemplating having a family. It allowed her to be her own boss and make her own hours and be in charge of her life. "It's tremendously stimulating work that is in a process of constant flux." It is an exciting career that allowed her to expand her options and gave her an opportunity to put her intellectual assertiveness, discipline, and logical and mathematical abilities to good use. "It does teach transferable skills and is a good payer, but it is difficult to deal with that wide cross section of humanity on a daily basis, which can make the strongest individual feel vulnerable." Roslyn remembers holding on to someone's trading jacket to keep herself from being physically swept away in the wave of human energy. The day came when a hefty 300-pounder stepped on her foot. That was it. Roslyn was ready for other challenges.

It was great fun while it lasted. Many days she couldn't wait to get on the floor. No two days were ever alike. She did it while she enjoyed it, until the day she asked herself, in the words of the Peggy Lee song, "Is that all there is?"

Roslyn feels she had the best of everything in quality and quantity. Yes, she would do it all over again. The next time, though, she would try harder to speak to Cary Grant!

# CHAPTER 16

# New Kid on the Block

JENNIFER COSTELLO

Jenny Costello belongs in this book because she is just starting out but has already accumulated an impressive list of accomplishments, including trading experience. She shares with the seasoned professionals a complex list of positive qualities that include a winning attitude and a belief in herself and her abilities to attain her desired goals. And the only thing "puffed up" about her is her basketball!

We met in the student lounge at the University of Chicago (U of C) where she is a fourth-year student majoring in psychology. My first impression was that she had her own personal energy reservoir. You could see it in her walk and her face. In fact, I made up a word to describe this quality: "Jenergy"! It's the fresh power of youth that she herself has generated by giving her utmost to her pursuits, which are considerable.

Jenny came to the U of C from a Catholic girls' school and describes her entire college experience as "amazing." She feels she has grown a great deal as a person. She has certainly made the most of the opportunities this prestigious and demanding school offers.

She is captain of the U of C women's varsity basketball team and president of the Women's Athletic Association. Jenny was also voted athlete-of-the-year and has held top academic standing in her class. It doesn't stop there. She is a licensed commodities broker who has traded futures successfully. She was also selected out of thousands of female college students nationwide to be one of *Glamour* magazine's "Top Ten College Women" for 1997. Jenny was selected on the basis of her remarkable goals, outstanding campus presence, demonstrated leadership ability, and academic excellence.

Jenny has enough goals to keep several energetic individuals occupied. She informed me that she would like to be part of a successful company, preferably her own, teach business, conduct motivational seminars for women (motivation is something she definitely knows and uses), write a book, and raise a family!

Her path to trading led through several summer jobs. Following her freshman year she worked as a telemarketer for the *New York Times*. In addition, her uncle, who also served as her basketball coach, invited her to work at the brokerage house where he is a partner. She observed, "This opportunity opened up a whole new world with which I had no familiarity. It was quite different from what I expected. I also found out that I liked it and was good at it too." She was drawn to its highly active atmosphere. As usual, she put all her energy into learning the brokerage business and moved up through the series of qualifying tests to a level where she was making decisions. This is not a person who is satisfied unless she demonstrates her best.

Jenny described her entry into brokerage and dealing with commodities as a process of learning a whole new language. Up to this point her entire experience had consisted of sports and academics and a busy schedule of volunteer work, committees, and getting into the National Honor Society. She was about to integrate a whole new field into her landscape. After her sophomore year she had a full-time summer job clerking, and she learned such basics as buying support and selling resistance. This appealed to her because, as she said, "I see myself as a people person interested in providing service."

It was not long before someone was absent on one of the busiest days, and Jenny was drafted to fill in and do his job. It sounds like a Katherine Hepburn movie. She admits she really "sweated" trading. She remembers one of her first real trades, a 100-lot of soybeans—on a par with her first ride on a two-wheeler or the first time her parents let her take the car by herself. "You get an extraordinary sense of independence and something in you changes forever." Jenny recalls it as a genuine smorgasbord learning experience. The S&P index has also made an impression on her! Overall, she learned a lot and also became committed to going on to learn more. Jenny is aware of the power of the financial markets and the extent of their domain.

Jenny reflected that trading on her own with her own money was a lot different! She took a $500 loss in bonds. "I freaked!" For Jenny this was serious money; "I didn't understand what happened, I was left with my mouth hanging open." Jenny lost no time in making it all back. She admits that the risk involved in trading for her own account still makes her a little bit nervous at this point.

Jenny's sports experience has helped in trading. Jenny understands the risk factor and is philosophical and practical in her appraisal: "You miss 100 percent of the shots you don't take!" She believes that "it is necessary to pick your battles and stick to your system based on technicals and fundamentals in a disciplined manner."

Often college summer jobs tend to be laid back: waitressing, a low-level office job, even camp counseling. Too often these aren't "real" jobs with real learning and responsibilities. Jenny was fortunate that she was the sort of person to take full advantage of the opportunity she was offered. It was not for nothing that she had earned the top academic position in her class. There was absolutely no question in her mind that she was going to go for it.

---

Jenny's sports experience has helped in trading.
Jenny understands the risk factor and is
philosophical and practical in her appraisal: "You
miss 100 percent of the shots you don't take!"

---

Jenny learned all she could about the fundamentals and technicals as well as the El Nino effect. Every day was different. She had become accustomed to a high-stress atmosphere in sports, and she recognized similarities in the action and sense of impending chaos that one is constantly trying to counteract by the right decisions in the market. Interestingly, Jenny thinks the most stressful days are actually the most fun days. There is so much going on and it's an opportunity to participate and have an effect. Most of all, crazy days are a great learning opportunity. It's like Lake Shore Drive during rush hour. You just navigate through the traffic until you reach your destination.

Jenny always tries to learn from her mistakes so she doesn't repeat the same ones and tries to maintain her sense of humor, which is a great antidote to stress and helps her to relate to her colleagues. Jenny also advises not letting a winner turn into a loser, something that can happen in a Chicago second.

Jenny's entire focus in anything she has chosen to do is to develop her gifts and talents. "I always strive to do my best. It's important for me to share my talents with others." She also has an extremely strong ethical sense, so she is as honest with others as she is with herself.

Jenny admits that trading grew on her. "I got into it and, somewhat to my surprise, enjoyed it." There was a lot more to "business" than she had thought. Actually, before she tried it she didn't know much except that she had pretty much ruled it out as a career possibility.

Jenny's work experience has taught her a lot. "I have found out that I do have a head for business and that I'm capable of making important, responsible decisions that affect other people. I genuinely enjoy interacting with clients, helping them make productive choices, and providing helpful information and financial guidance." She is a "people person" and not a number cruncher.

Jenny was the only woman and the youngest employee at the firm, but this was neither a hindrance nor an obstacle to her learning and advancement. One of the reasons for her self-confidence has been her family. She is the eldest of four children in an Irish-Polish family. Two of her siblings are in college and one is still in high school. Her dad sells insurance and her mom is a first-grade teacher. She describes her family as incredibly close and "everything to me." Jenny says they support her in every way and believe in her. One senses that this bond is an incredible source of strength and energy for her as it must be for them.

One of Jenny's earlier work experiences had been as coach and director of a basketball camp. Basketball is her game. She loves it and has learned a great deal more than basketball from it. In the past, she has also played softball and soccer and is currently picking up golf to fill in the chinks. Her tightly packed life always has room for volunteering for a wide range of activities, including the Special Olympics.

In her work as in her academics and sports, Jenny pushes herself to the limit, no matter what. Her philosophy sounds like a line from a fairy tale, but this one has come true and is real: "Do whatever you need to make your dreams come true." Jenny's deep religious convictions are also a solid source of inner strength and personal inspiration. Jenny genuinely feels she is on this earth to serve, share, and help others. It is as if she is on a "mission possible" of excellence and accomplishment.

—————  ▬▬  —————

Jenny genuinely feels she is on this earth to serve,

share, and help others. It is as if she is on a "mission

possible" of excellence and accomplishment. "What

helps me is trying to keep things in perspective. I'll

take risks but they are calculated risks."

———————

"What helps me is trying to keep things in perspective. I'll take risks but they are calculated risks." She is disciplined without being rigid and is intelligently active. She tries to take things as they come and to learn from down days. She feels incredibly fortunate to have succeeded in so many areas. One area seems to nourish another. It's like motivational cross-pollination.

Jenny does have some basic rules. "I believe in living each day to the fullest with my faith as my guide." She consistently does the best with what she has been given. Jenny always helps her teammates. She is still trying to find her place in business but is off to a great start. Jenny has had a lot of attractive offers to choose from and has accepted a position at the Chicago office of Goldman Sachs. When we last talked, she had been written about on the front page of *The Wall Street Journal* as well as the Sunday edition of the *Chicago Tribune* and had been selected to be on the USA All-Academic team.

It wasn't difficult for Jenny to recall a memorable moment. It occurred when she traded the yen. It was a winner. Her plan had worked. She also realized that she couldn't expect a winner every day. Just as in basketball, "you win some and you lose some." "Trading," Jenny speculates, "is knowing how to assume calculated risk."

A down market when you are on the long side is definitely a down moment, but that doesn't mean you have to go down with it. Jenny remembers a losing trade in bonds that she managed to turn into a winner. It was a valuable experience and taught her that it's always essential to have a way to get out of a losing trade or position. It is very important to refrain from beating yourself up as "you need the womanpower to keep on going forward."

Losing periods in the market are like the last five minutes of the last quarter when the other team has the ball. They are opportunities for learning and turning things around. When everything is going as planned, you are usually just enjoying riding the wave. It is these challenging times that require resourcefulness and inventiveness to foster learning. "At these times," Jenny adds, "your analysis usually doesn't quite match what you're confronting. The key you've been given doesn't fit. The solution is up to you!" Jenny has experienced hard times and gets through them by sticking to her plan while being flexible. "Discipline will get you through. It's so easy to just cave in."

Jenny judges success as a good day when she is able to use all the things she has learned. In terms of trading, this means having the discipline to stick with her system. She also tries to put everything she has learned at the client's service. Of course, making money doesn't hurt!

Jenny described her colleagues at the "MAD Group Investments" as a great caring group of people who have fun while working hard. Jenny views them as a basketball team and herself as a member. She is very firm in not doing anything she doesn't believe in. "My clients deserve the best and with me they are going to get it!"

As far as needing to be in control, Jenny likes having a leadership role but definitely doesn't see herself as a control freak. She does like to have a plan but knows she has to expect the unexpected. She enjoys surprises. They keep her alert and ready. In general, she feels she knows how to play the game on the court and in the office.

She sees herself assuming many different roles. She is outgoing and enjoys taking on a lot of varied responsibilities. She's a student and an athlete during the school year. In the summer months she becomes a business person whose main objective is helping clients make wise decisions. She is also a member of a family, a daughter, a friend. Jenny fills each of her many roles fully. She is always giving her all and doing her best in this "bright mosaic," as she describes her life of relationships.

Jenny knows that in trading things can change in an instant and security is a concept that is extremely short lived. Unlike basketball, with trading it's not over even when the bell rings if you have a position.

No matter what happens, Jenny's methods in life extend to her trading practices. She looks for the positive side. Jenny also watches for "double bottoms" or "double tops" as well as places where fundamentals and technicals meet and are pointing in the same direction. She has a solid knowledge of the industry and talks with ease and conviction about its nature and behavior. It's important to remember she is a psychology major and tends to go beyond the obvious to the underlying contributing structures.

Although Jenny always tries to be disciplined and stick to her plan based on her analysis of technicals and fundamentals, she does admit to having a daring side, as any good trader must. The responsible, calculated risk side has to provide stability and security for the daring leaps.

Jenny takes decision making very seriously and tries to consider all the options before making her selection. It's not easy because she does like to be right. She admits that sometimes she feels she thinks too much. Laughing, she revealed that she has a really terrible time making a decision when she's shopping for jeans!

Jenny describes herself as "extremely competitive." As the captain of the basketball team and athlete of the year, she says she is completely different on the court. She becomes incredibly intense and turns into a tigress! I could see it! "I believe in playing hard but fair and competing against myself." These are qualities that she can put into play in trading and in making successful recommendations to clients.

She has never felt intimidated on the court or in the office. Not only was she the only woman in the office, she was considerably younger than any of her colleagues and customers. She didn't let this stop her but simply viewed it as an opportunity to show them what she could do. "It was a chance to excel." She tends to accept advice not as criticism but as the words of a coach who is interested in helping her improve her game—on the court or in the office.

How does she do what she does? Jenny's strength comes from her family and her faith. Whether in her summer office role or as a member of a winning basketball team, she sees herself as part of something larger and doing her utmost to help her group or team. She sees her participation as one of strengthening the overall effort. On the court or in the office, as in life, every day is different. There is constant energy and constant change and she has to be ready to interact with it.

For someone as positive, prepared, and bright as Jenny, losing is tough. She doesn't like to lose money or lose in general. When it does happen, she looks at her decision to see if there was anything else she could have done. She also keeps in mind that no system is perfect and she values learning from mistakes. Jenny does try to avoid those "could haves" and "should haves" and instead uses a negative situation as a stepping stone to understanding so it won't happen again, at least not exactly the same way.

Jenny views her activity-packed life as a whole ball of wax. She believes that "trading and sports have a lot to teach about life to anyone willing to learn." She has learned the value of working hard, being dedicated to learning and staying goal oriented. It's important to maintain an optimistic outlook even when there doesn't seem much to support it. Jenny is of the opinion that there is always a new market or a new way of looking at an old market. She tries to keep things in perspective but also brings a fresh perspective into play. If it doesn't go her way, she's learned that it's not the end of the world. She tries to use her sense of humor and honesty at all times.

Jenny does admit that she is extremely hard on herself and has to remind herself that it is very important to go out and just have fun! Like anyone else her age, she enjoys dancing and just hanging out with her diverse group of friends. She likes concerts and "oldies." She finds shooting hoops relaxing and also tries to keep up with her diary.

When asked what she thought about comparing trading to sex or war, as so many men do, she thought that it was a "male thing." Jenny sees trading more as an activity that requires preparation, planning, and total mental focus. Even then it's a win some/lose some game.

As someone relatively new to the trading game, she has "lots of advice"! First on her long list is the recommendation to be receptive and keep your eyes open to what's out there, and a lot is. Next, soak up everything: fundamentals, technicals, pricing strategies. Also keep in mind what works for you and try to work with a mentor. Be patient and stick with your strategy through the learning process, which is long and complex and can be frustrating. "Don't get discouraged. No one can become a good ball player or trader overnight." Work the audit track to practice without risking real money. Be really disciplined; stick to your guns, stick to your plan, and restrict yourself to one or two markets. You can't be master of the universe but you can sure earn a corner you can call your own. The last piece of advice is just as important as all that precedes it: Have fun!

When she has children, Jenny would encourage them to try trading if they had the right teacher and perspective. She would like them to learn how to invest but also reflects that it is a dangerous and uncertain business. Any firm they want to join should have high standards of integrity.

Jenny feels she has gotten a great deal out of her trading experience. Every day has been different and has presented opportunities for her to use her intellectual and athletic sides in tandem. "I like making money and using money to make money."

She sees a lot of potential in the business world. What she hasn't liked has been losing money and not being able to prevent a client from making a mistake. She doesn't like to see anyone pour money on a loser. Jenny is genuinely enthusiastic about her work and wants her clients to enjoy the process as much as she does.

Jenny observed that her brokerage and trading experience has taught her a great deal about the world and how things are interconnected. As an example, she mentioned the ripples from El Nino's effect on the midwest's corn crop. Jenny has discovered that she was stronger and more capable than she had previously thought. She has shown herself that she can develop a good plan and follow it with successful results. She feels she is in a better position to pursue her goals than she was before. She reminds me to mention that her trading profits helped pay for her senior year tuition.

Jenny has developed a powerful combination of hard work and an outlook on life with her sense of playing a part in something bigger. She is extremely honest and open and admits she enjoys trading a lot. She senses there is a lot of potential for her even though she finds it "a bit scary"! Jenny especially enjoys working with people and developing better and more successful plans and winning strategies.

Jenny wears a special medal dedicated to Saint Dymphna, the patron saint of worriers. It was a gift from her parents. Jenny takes good care of herself, so that I can't help thinking that Saint Dymphna has a very easy job. Jenny is her own lucky charm!

# Through the
# Looking Glass

We've met 15 remarkable women and examined each one's life well enough to feel we actually know them. They've taken us along on their journey, not slowing down or sparing any hardship, but guiding us in their footsteps and pointing out the dangers as well as the exhilarating parts. As Alice found out, things got "curiouser and curiouser"; she had to be alert and confident.

Each woman is absolutely authentic, each story unique. Each woman participates fully in life. Nobody settles for less than the "best." And best in the sense of what suited the soul and the spirit, not in the sense of luxurious or costly. Sometimes there were delays and sacrifices but the goal was always beaming them in. Their paths read like a well-wrinkled, much folded, smudgy map indicating unexpected detours in intermediate jobs or rearing children, entering the trading portals of the markets with the trepidation of Dorothy as she arrived at Oz. Like Dorothy, no matter what manner of flying monkeys and delays they experienced, each was as determined as a salmon to reach her goal.

Each woman participates fully in life. Nobody settles

for less than the "best." And best in the sense of what

suited the soul and the spirit, not in the sense of

luxurious or costly.

In some cases the path led from the suburbs, which can present their own daunting obstacles of comfort, security, and predictability of an easier daily existence away from turmoil and pressure. Each woman is a living illustration of the saying, "The road to success is always under construction!"

Everybody made it taking her own route and using her own individual methods. Each developed a way of responding to the various exchanges' culture of sights, sounds, and smells in a teeming and vibrant financial world-affecting and world-affected ritual.

Ann Berg traveled through Dante's *Inferno* by means of her art, constructing with light faint as from distant stars in the sometimes impenetrable darkness, gathering the light into ever-increasing areas of clarity and understanding. She was always looking beyond the surface, reading the layers to arrive at an understanding of the fundamental structure in order to explain its complex character and seeming contradictory behavior. In a way, she was always engaged in the process of skinning ever larger and thicker-hided muskrats that guarded the halls of darkness. Anyone who has been in the Chicago Board of Trade's new building knows *its* glass ceiling is dizzyingly high. Ann made it to *her* glass ceiling and shattered it by means of her knowledge, climbing with eyes and hands slowly to the top.

Mickey Norton never doubted herself and waded right through that sea of men with determination and focus on her goal. Her support and involvement with the championship Bulls is completely understandable as a kindred enterprise to trading. It's a hard act to follow and leaves an enduring expectation of what life should be.

Carol Hancock had a strong sense of personal right. She was not about to be an absentee seat holder. She was determined to exercise her right to trade and she wasn't going to let anyone keep her from doing what she had set her mind to. She took on an exclusive group almost as large as her hometown. It was for a time like the standoff in the movie *High Noon*. She was not going to go away. She had her membership in the CBOT and was going to exercise her right to use it. Carol prevailed, not because she hired an attorney or gathered a support group around her. She made it because she stood her ground and kept learning. She was not about to undergo a sex change operation to fit the traditional profile of the trader as a male!

Robin Mesch's glass ceiling is on the screen before her. It is a membrane covered with critical information that she must decode in daily confrontations in order to unlock its secrets. All of this needs to be done in a race against the fish whose gleaming teeth serve as a graphic warning: Don't get caught; wait for your signal!

In Karen Doherty's case, the glass ceiling needed cleaning. She barely gave it a glance as she entered and participated in the male trading culture. Coming from a large, brother-filled family, this seemed like a variation of what she recognized. Her family is first and as a single professional mom she makes a good living and can take care of her kids without worrying.

Leslie Henner Burns had a lot of options but was just going to show her family she could handle the "family business." She is confident that her husband is handling things at home and she's got the best possible child care provider!

Arlene Busch thrives on risk, prefers to be on the edge, and has exchanged the glass ceiling for Baccarat crystal, the only kind worth having at her level. She absolutely runs on risk. If there is no risk involved, don't bother Arlene!

Mary MacDiarmid enjoys finding peace and humor in financial jeopardy. With her height of six feet, Mary's attitude about ceilings is that she has to be careful not to bump her head!

Sharon King was not used to glass ceilings. Low, cracked ones with some dangling insulation were more like it. She was going to get through to make sure she had the kind of life she wanted—her own not someone else's idea of "no life at all."

Janet Disteldorf found a strange version of dance and theater on the trading floor. She saw the trading rites as compelling and dramatic as any stage performance and saw herself reflected in their script and message. The name of her long-running spectacle is "Independence Day"!

Katherine Harig started out with the fledgling S&P index and has stuck by it on its thundering flight into the future. She didn't pick this market for comfort or glamour but because it was the place where she had an opportunity to compete and achieve her high goals for herself.

Jennifer Strausberg designs her own glass "windshield" from elements gathered from her vast network. No two panes are alike, but her design works and is a marvel to behold, seemingly in a constant state of motion like a glass mobile. She is always tinkering with it, adding a new piece or an ancient shard from a dig.

Roslyn Abell sees science everywhere and physics in particular. Little did Newton know one of his laws would be applied to trading! Physics seeks to unlock the secrets of the larger universe and, in Roslyn's experience, can be put to work explaining the behavior of the trading universe and its "market mind." Roslyn's first instinct when encountering any glass ceiling is to analyze its physical properties and assess its structural strengths and weaknesses.

Mei Ping Yang's glass is of celadon purity. It requires scrupulous care and research to identify its unique properties, verify its authenticity, and use its ancient wisdom in the modern world. She has taken on the imperial five-clawed dragon that represents the foreign currency markets she moves about in with willowlike enduring strength and flexibility. For her, the glass ceiling is an opening in a complex temple of finance chimes with information gathered by bells from the world's far financial corners!

Jenny Costello is fully capable of bounding up to the glass, which she expects to reach and shatter, by diligent practice and energized intelligence. She shares with all the women the characteristics of personal strength and indomitable belief in her ability to stay the course until the ball goes "swish" through the hoop.

———————————————

The personal DNA that each of these women possesses and exhibits is a strong upward spiral of discipline, focus, self-confidence, and steadfast optimism. No matter what was thrown at them, there was no question that each would pick herself up or hang on to a trading coat to avoid being swept away.

————

The personal DNA that each of these women possesses and exhibits is a strong upward spiral of discipline, focus, self-confidence, and steadfast optimism. No matter what was thrown at them, there was no question that each would pick herself up or hang on to a trading coat to avoid being swept away. Each demonstrates the words of a young Russian Olympian that you first have to be a champion in your own mind. To succeed after many years of practicing to be exquisitely good at something, it's necessary to be your own toughest coach as well as your own biggest fan! So what if what you have your heart set on resembles someone jumping out of a plane without a parachute. It may appear foolish or even suicidal except that you know where to catch those breezes with eagle-eyed focus, calculation, and maneuverability.

All the women went "into the woods." Each one left her previous locale as if following a call only she could hear. They all gathered around the "camp circles" that are like the cells composing the world's economic life. The hot energetic center of the market's volcaniclike character pulled them toward itself. The volcano image is an appropriate one for the amorphous energy that is barely captured under the market umbrella. Sometimes it is as serene as a pleasant hillside waiting for unsuspecting picnickers. At other times, deep rumblings suggest hidden danger and imbalance. The extreme case occurs when the whole thing blows and those on its financial flanks are swept away by its lava or suffocated by lingering gases. There are a few difficult-to-understand individuals known as "volcano lovers." All good traders seem to have more or less of the quality of risk seeking. Each one of the women described in the preceding pages would have excelled at whatever career choice she made. It is interesting that they all pursued such a demanding and unforgiving goal.

It is one thing to reach the goal. The real work comes in hanging on to the glass ceiling, not giving up, and ultimately penetrating it by knowledge, experience, and sheer sense of self. Endurance comes from doing those continuous laps in choppy, chilly waters, not from lounging around a warm turquoise pool!

Not one woman measures success in terms of worldly goods. Money is the means of keeping score but not the driving force. Each person I met lives a balanced existence. I found each a reflective, philosophical person who knows herself extremely well. Not in the New Age or therapy sense but in the sense of each life being well examined and well lived. Each woman gave articulate, honest testimony to her trials.

This band of pioneers, because that is what they are in all shapes, colors, ages, and backgrounds, do not appear particularly tough at first glance. They tend to be low key, solid, not "puffed up" or self-absorbed. But if you look into their eyes, you see that clear unflinching gaze—steady, cool, and undistracted. If you hear their words, you understand that their firm convictions, their knowledge, and their experience-based careers are as strong as steel constructed bridges and towers of dizzying height. Their inner structures are also as simple and flexible as an Indian teepee, whose stakes can be collapsed with umbrella ease and moved to a safer hunting ground.

In each case, they exhibit a burning desire to pass through the glass to get closer to the volcano! There is no peace without winning the battle or the contest. In whichever way they viewed their environment—as a pit of unruly boys or an orchestra hall—each maintained an image of herself that no one and nothing else could alter. Any change had to come from the person in charge of her life: herself.

---

They all have an extraordinary need for

independence and realize that, like the free

enterprise system in which they have participated, it

is achieved by individual drive and purposeful effort.

---

They all have an extraordinary need for independence and realize that, like the free enterprise system in which they have participated, it is achieved by individual drive and purposeful effort. Their concept of freedom is work based and unrelenting. Freedom isn't given. It's earned and needs daily re-creation. Life continues every day and requires full and genuine participation or you aren't even going to get near that glass ceiling! Speaking of the ceiling that appears in various guises and heights, it seems to me it is a psychological barrier that only appears real. It is somewhat like the screen the Great Oz hid behind. The point is not to be so preoccupied with the ceiling, giving it false importance. No one in this book started a Glass Ceiling Study Group or relied on legal measures or claims of harassment.

I would like to borrow Roslyn Abell's comparison of the various commodities to music. Each of these inspirational women possesses a strong tone, her unique "voice," that beams and keeps her directed toward her goal. Janet's ten minutes of Melencamp, Roslyn's penchant for the country-and-western sound of Garth Brooks, Sharon's "I Can Fly" from *The Lion King* stream alongside Ann's Italian baroque music and the purity of the Gregorian chanting that Mei Ping favors. There is also the strong percussive, life-affirming sound of Mickey Norton's Bulls "Victory Chant" and the quieter, lyrical, Celtic strains of Karen Doherty. Mary is recharged by the peace of Carole King's words. Jenny hangs out with "oldies"! Leslie plays the piano alongside her children. World music would be an appropriate choice for Arlene Busch. I can see Carol as a story song performed with a strong but light touch. Jennifer listens to jazz while doing as many things at once as possible. Robin suggests the complex classical piano works that she once devoted herself to and is considering returning to at this point in her life. Katherine has her car stocked with everything from Peter, Paul and Mary to Metallica! All of their sounds flow and rise together in one thunderous "Ode to Joy," lifting that glass ceiling right off! They have all given their full measure to their life. We are strengthened by their stories.

---

They have all given their full measure to their life. We are strengthened by their stories.

# Glossary

**arbitrage**  The simultaneous purchase and sale of similar financial instruments or commodity futures in order to benefit from an anticipated change in their price relationship.

**backwardation**  A condition where the nearby (close to expiration) futures months and spot prices are at a premium to the deferred (farther to expiration) months.

**bid**  Indicates a willingness to purchase a futures contract at a specific price.

**buy an opening**  To buy at the beginning of a trading session at a price within the opening range.

**buy in**  To cover, offset, or close out a short position.

**buy on close**  To buy at the end of the trading session at a price within the closing range.

**car**  A loose quantity term sometimes used to describe a contract (e.g., car of bellies). Derived from the fact that quantities of the product specified in a contract used to correspond closely to the capacity of a railroad car.

**cash commodity**  The actual physical commodity as distinguished from a futures contract.

**CFTC**  The Commodity Futures Trading Commission, the federal agency created by Congress to regulate futures trading.

**clearing house**  An adjunct to a futures exchange through which transactions executed on the floor of the exchange are settled using a process of matching purchases and sales. A clearing organization is also charged with the proper conduct of delivery procedures and the adequate financing of the entire operation.

**clearing member**  A member firm of the clearing house. Each clearing member must also be a member of the Exchange. Not all members of the Exchange are members of the clearing organization. All trades of a nonclearing member must be registered with, and eventually settled through, a clearing member.

**close**   The period at the end of the trading session; sometimes used to refer to the closing price.

**closing price (or range)**   The high and low prices, or bids and offers, recorded during the period designated as the official close.

**commission**   The one-time fee normally charged by a broker to a customer when a futures or options position is liquidated either by offset or delivery.

**contract**   A unit of trading for a financial or commodity future. Also, the actual agreement between the buyer and a seller of a transaction as defined by an exchange.

**contract month**   The month in which futures contracts may be satisfied by making or accepting a delivery.

**cover**   The purchase of a contract to offset a previously established short position.

**day trading**   Refers to establishing and liquidating the same position or positions within one day's trading.

**deck**   The floor broker's stack of orders awaiting execution.

**delivery**   The tender and receipt of an actual commodity or financial instrument in settlement of a futures contract.

**derivatives**   Financial contracts whose value changes with, or is derived from, price movements in an underlying financial instrument, such as a stock, bond, or commodity.

**discretionary account**   All accounts over which an individual or organization, other than the person in whose name the account is carried, exercises trading authority or control.

**double bottom**   Describes a situation when the market retests a previous low.

**double top**   Describes a situation when the market retests a previous high.

**floor broker**   A member, licensed by the CFTC, who is paid a fee for executing orders for the clearing members or their customers.

**futures contract**   Standardized, transferable agreement to buy or sell a financial instrument or commodity at a specific point in the future at a price determined when the agreement is made.

**liquidity**   The market is liquid when it has a high level of trading activity (i.e., buying and selling with minimum price disturbance).

**long** One who has bought a contract or contracts to establish a market position and who has not yet closed out this position through an offsetting sale; the opposite of short.

**market maker** An individual who provides bid and offer in the market.

**opening** The period at the beginning of the trading session officially designated by the Exchange during which all transaction are considered made "at the opening."

**open outcry** The continuous auction process in which bids and offers on the trading floor are made and accepted out loud.

**option** An instrument giving the purchaser the right, but not the obligation, to buy ("call" options) or sell ("put" options) a fixed amount of a given asset at a specific price on or before a certain expiration date.

**pit** A specific area of the trading floor designated for the trading of an individual futures or options contract.

**position** An interest in the market, either long or short, in the form of open contract.

**premium** The price of an options contract; also, in futures trading, the amount by which the futures price exceeds the price of the spot commodity.

**put** An option granting the right to sell the underlying futures contract.

**runner** Employee of a clearing firm who "runs" market orders from the order desk into the pit.

**scalp** To trade for small gains. It normally involves establishing and liquidating a position quickly, usually within the same day.

**settlement price** A figure determined by the closing range used to calculate gains and losses in the future market accounts.

**short** One who has sold a contract to establish a market position and who has not yet closed out this position through an offsetting purchase; the opposite of long.

**speculator** One who attempts to anticipate price changes and, through buying and selling contracts, aims to make profits.

**spread** Refers to the simultaneous purchase and sale of contracts for the same commodity or instrument for delivery in different months, or in different but related markets.

**tick** The smallest price change up or down.

**volume** The number of transactions in a futures contract or options on futures contract made during a specified period time.